J. M. Synge's *The Playboy of the Western World*

T0383391

'I'm thinking this night wasn't I a foolish fellow not to kill my father in years gone by.'

– Christy Mahon

On the first night of **J. M. Synge's** *The Playboy of the Western World* (1907), the audience began protesting in the theatre; by the third night the protests had spilled onto the streets of Dublin. How did one play provoke this? Christopher Collins addresses *The Playboy*'s satirical treatment of illusion and realism in light of Ireland's struggle for independence, as well as Synge's struggle for artistic expression. By exploring Synge's unpublished diaries, drafts and notebooks, he seeks to understand how and why the play came to be.

This volume invites the reader behind the scenes of this inflammatory play and its first performances, to understand how and why Synge risked everything in the name of art.

Christopher Collins is Assistant Professor of Drama at Nottingham University.

The Fourth Wall

The Fourth Wall series is a growing collection of short books on famous plays. Its compact format perfectly suits the kind of fresh, engaging criticism that brings a play to life.

Each book in this series selects one play or musical as its subject and approaches it from an original angle, seeking to shed light on an old favourite or break new ground on a modern classic. These lively, digestible books are a must for anyone looking for new ideas on the major works of modern theatre.

Also available in this series:

Heiner Müller's *The Hamletmachine* by David Barnett
Lerner and Loewe's *My Fair Lady* by Keith Garebian
Samuel Beckett's *Krapp's Last Tape* by Daniel Sack
Thornton Wilder's *The Skin of Our Teeth* by Kyle Gillette
Harold Pinter's *Party Time* by Graham White

Coming soon:

Georg Büchner's *Woyzeck* by Karoline Gritzner
Benjamin Britten's *Peter Grimes* by Sam Kinchin-Smith
J. M. Barrie's *Peter Pan* by Lucie Sutherland
Sondheim and Wheeler's *Sweeney Todd* by Aaron Thomas
Errol John's *Moon on a Rainbow Shawl* by Lynnette Goddard
Caryl Churchill's *Far Away* by Dan Rebellato
August Wilson's *Joe Turner's Come and Gone* by Ladrica Menson-Furr
Tim Crouch's *An Oak Tree* by Catherine Love
Rogers and Hammerstein's *The Sound of Music* by Julian Woolford

J. M. Synge's *The Playboy of the Western World*

Christopher Collins

Routledge
Taylor & Francis Group

LONDON AND NEW YORK

First published 2016
by Routledge
2 Park Square, Milton Park, Abingdon, Oxon OX14 4RN

and by Routledge
711 Third Avenue, New York, NY 10017

Routledge is an imprint of the Taylor & Francis Group, an informa business

British Library Cataloguing-in-Publication Data
A catalogue record for this book is available from
the British Library

Library of Congress Cataloguing-in-Publication Data
A catalog record for this title has been requested

ISBN: 9781138194694 (pbk)
ISBN: 9781315638720 (ebk)

Typeset in Bembo
by Out of House Publishing

For Céline Christine Lehmann, with love.

Contents

Acknowledgements

I am grateful to the various keepers of manuscripts at the Berg Collection and Foster-Murphy Collection in the New York Public Library and the National Library of Ireland, and, above all, to the keepers of manuscripts at Trinity College, Dublin.

I am thankful to my colleagues and students at the Department of Drama, Trinity College, Dublin, for their invaluable support in helping me think through the research presented in this book, especially Melissa Sihra, Eric Weitz and Brian Singleton.

Thank you to my editors at Routledge, Ben Piggott and Kate Edwards for your continued support.

Thank you to Mary Caulfield; Paul Murphy; Ben Murnane; Justin and Jane MacGregor; Nicholas and Emily Johnson; Professor Anthony Roche; Gabriel Graham; James Hickson; Ann Mulligan and Rhona Greene; Jack Jeffery; Deirdre and John Heath; Eibhlin and Peter Colgan; and Margaret, Michael and Tom Roche for challenging and supporting my thinking on Synge's plays and performances. A very special thank to Neasa ní Chuanaigh for explaining Synge's Hiberno-Irish dialect to me.

Thank you to my family, Lesley and Desmond, William and Hannah Collins for all of your love and support.

My dearest thanks to Céline Christine Lehmann. This book is for you.

Christopher Collins
Southwold

Abbreviations

Note: all quotations from manuscript collections, and Synge's *Collected Works* and *Collected Letters* preserve original spelling.

CL, Vol. I	J. M. Synge, *The Collected Letters of John Millington Synge*. Vol. I, *1871–1907*. Ed. Ann Saddlemyer. Oxford: Clarendon Press, 1983.
CW, Vol. II	J. M. Synge, *Collected Works*. Vol. II, *Prose*. Ed. Alan Price. London: Oxford University Press, 1966.
CW, Vol. IV	J. M. Synge, *Collected Works*. Vol. IV, *Plays*, Book II. Ed. Ann Saddlemyer. Gerrards Cross: Colin Smythe, 1982.
NLI MS	National Library of Ireland Manuscript
NYPL MS	New York Public Library Manuscript
TCD MS	Manuscripts of the Irish Literary Renaissance: J. M. Synge Manuscripts from the Library of Trinity College Dublin.
TCD SSMS	Stephens–Synge Manuscripts from the Library of Trinity College Dublin.

Introduction

John Millington Synge is one the most important and most influential playwrights in modern theatre. Born in 1871 in Dublin, Ireland, Synge had a professional career as a playwright that lasted just seven years before his untimely death at the age of 37. However, his direct influence on subsequent generations of playwrights is quite outstanding: Antonin Artaud, Bertolt Brecht, Federico García Lorca, Eugene O'Neill, Samuel Beckett, Brian Friel and Marina Carr have all publicly stated how much they are indebted to Synge. The pinnacle of his career as playwright came on 26 January 1907 when he premiered his satirical comedy *The Playboy of the Western World* at the Abbey Theatre in Dublin.[1] On that infamous evening the audience were absolutely appalled by what they saw and heard, so much so that they began causing disturbances that lasted for an almost an entire week.

This book explores how and why Synge wrote *The Playboy of the Western World*. The play is first placed in the context of the Ireland of Synge's time. The next two chapters offer a textual and thematic analysis of the play and an analysis of its performance history. A key aspect of this book is to explore

Synge's and his Abbey Theatre colleagues' diaries, notebooks and letters so that we can understand their private thoughts on the play and the performance. It is hoped that by consulting the archive a richer, and maybe even an alternative, understanding of the play can be ascertained.

The Playboy of the Western World is a play about the problems of believing in illusions. The play is set in a small rural community in north County Mayo, on Ireland's west coast. Into this community arrives the play's protagonist, Christopher 'Christy' Mahon. Christy is the shy, underachieving son of Old Mahon. Christy has arrived in Mayo from County Kerry, approximately 270 km south from Mayo along the Irish west coast. Frightened and exhausted, he stumbles into a shebeen (an illicit pub) claiming that he has fled his native Kerry because he has just committed patricide: the murder of his father. Instead of running for the police and the priest (which was what the first audiences expected), the community is fascinated by Christy's bravery. He is promptly offered a job working as a pot-boy (waiter) in the shebeen by its owner, Michael James Flaherty. Christy accepts and, with a now ever-growing confidence, he woos Michael James's fearless daughter, Margaret 'Pegeen Mike' Flaherty, with some wonderfully poetic, deeply romantic lines: 'Isn't there the light of seven heavens in your heart alone, the way you'll be an angel's lamp to me.'[2] Pegeen Mike may be engaged to the timid, God-fearing Shawn Keogh, but she is happy to entertain thoughts of marrying Christy because she finds Shawn weak-willed in comparison. Having won Pegeen Mike's heart, Christy is totally transformed into the playboy of the western world (the western world being an index for the west of Ireland). Christy can do no wrong. However, when Old Mahon quite surprisingly arrives in the shebeen searching for his son, both the community and Christy suddenly realise that everyone has been living an illusory life. Desperate to keep a hold of the illusion Christy attempts to kill his father in reality. Now, the illusion of patricide is coming alarmingly real, and Christy almost succeeds in killing his father. Shocked and appalled with what is happening in front of their eyes, Pegeen leads the community in taking justice into their own hands. She and others proceed to torture Christy before turning him over to the police. At the height of the torturing, a badly injured Old Mahon comes back into the shebeen. Michael James apologises for torturing Christy and the Mahons promptly leave the community. As life returns to reality Christy realises that he has seen a glimpse of his real potential from living an illusory life; no longer will he be the shy, underachieving son. Pegeen Mike, however, is left devastated with the thoughts of what could have been if the illusion had never been broken. She is brought crashing back down to earth, knowing that she has lost the playboy of the western world and, furthermore, that she is still engaged to Shawn Keogh.

Why is this play still relevant?

In 2009 the *Irish Times* decided to look back on the first decade of theatre in the new millennium. They stated that the 'defining play of the decade was actually written in 1907' and concluded that *The Playboy of the Western World* is an 'ever-contemporary masterpiece'.[3] *The Playboy of the Western World* is relevant today for three main reasons. First, it exposes the problems of believing in illusions. This is why one of the most quoted lines from the play is Pegeen Mike's 'there's a great gap between a gallous story and a dirty deed'.[4] What she means by this is that Christy's story of how he killed his father might be one thing, but actually going through with the reality of killing your father is quite another.

Second, it is a comic masterpiece of modern theatre. *The Playboy* was heavily influenced by the work of two French comic writers: Molière and François Rabelais. Synge explores the problems of believing in illusions by dramatising stereotypical characters that speak in a fast-paced, wonderfully lyrical language (Synge's debt to Molière), and at the same time the play is ruthlessly satirical (his debt to Rabelais).

The third reason the play is relevant today is because it is a testament to the importance of artistic expression. In January 1907 the difference between illusion and reality went far beyond the Abbey Theatre and turned the streets, the newspapers and the courtrooms into a theatre with just as much drama as Synge's play. Spectators simply couldn't believe that Synge would have the audacity to satirise Irish life. Turning to the diary of the architect of the Abbey Theatre, Joseph Holloway, we can see just how shocking Synge's new play was. Holloway wrote:

> What did Synge mean by such filth? Was there no one to supervise the plays? Synge met with his just deserts from the audience & I hope he'll take the lesson to heart. This is not Irish life? . . . I maintain that this play of The Playboy is not a truthful or just picture of the Irish peasants, but simply the outpouring of a morbid, unhealthy mind ever seeking on the dungheep of life for the nastiness that lies concealed there, perhaps, but never suspected by the clean of mind . . . Synge is the evil genius of the Abbey . . . the theatre is forever damned in the eyes of all right thinking Irishmen.[5]

What Synge encountered during the first performances is quite unlike anything that we would expect from going to the theatre today. Members of the audience stomped their feet, whistled, sang, cheered, booed and generally made as much noise as they could in order to stop the play from being performed, and demanded that Synge make himself known. Synge attended all of the performances of *The Playboy* but the vast majority of the disturbers did not know what he looked like, and so night after night they aggressively howled, 'We want the author.'[6] Just imagine sitting in a theatre with 561 other people knowing that the vast majority of them are so upset with you that they have turned violent with each other. For example, a newspaper reports how during the fourth performance of the play:

> a low-sized Englishman in the stalls, who was an upholder of the play, got into an altercation with a young gentleman in the pit who entertained diametrically opposite views. At length, the former challenged the latter to fight him. The gage of battle was at once taken up. Followed by a couple of hundred persons the combatants made their ways into the vestibule. Here several blows were exchanged.[7]

Synge refused to back down. In the newspapers he claimed that 'we simply claimed the liberty of art to choose what subjects we think to fit to put on'.[8] Both Christy in the play and Synge in real life were subject to the anger of those who took the illusion of art far too faithfully. The imaginary community in Mayo and the real-life spectators in Dublin did not see art as a subjective perspective on reality with the ability to inspire and challenge real life, but as a wicked trick that brought their whole world crashing down. Throughout this book we will see how, in defending the play, Synge continually uses the word 'reality' to argue his case. 'On the stage one must have reality, and one must have joy', Synge believed.[9] The problem was that his understanding of reality and joy was not considered to be artistic in the slightest. What the play calls into question, then, is the value of poetic license; freedom of speech; the importance of satire; and ultimately, the importance of artistic expression.

These three key points – (1) the problems with believing in illusions, (2) the play's comic strategies and (3) the importance of artistic expression – will be continually returned to throughout this book, because not only do they link how and why Synge wrote the play and how the play was received in performance both then and throughout history, but significantly they also demonstrate why a play from 1907 is still relevant today. At the time of writing, the western world is still reeling after the *Charlie Hebdo* attacks in Paris in January 2015, where masked gunmen attacked and killed the editor and three cartoonists of the French satirical magazine. And while what happened in Paris can never be directly compared to the disturbances that greeted *The Playboy*, the principle remains that *The Playboy* is contemporary today because it is a play about the integrity of art. The fact that the second performance of the play was performed under police guard becomes a parable for the importance of art in the face of oppression. All art, be it Christy's poetical story about killing his father or Synge's satirical play about an imagined community in County Mayo, should always be seen as a 'gallous story' rather than a 'dirty deed.' Art may have sincere and often political consequences for the real world, but the act of creation should always be seen as a world of make-believe before it is seen as a world of make-believe. The problem, then, is with taking art too literally. And this is the problem with the most pervasive form of art there is: realism.

Realism

Right at the heart of *The Playboy* are the problems inherent with realism. Realism falsely claims to be an objective study of 'real' life. However, realism is entirely subjective and, more often than not, it persuades the spectator into having empathy with the dominant understanding of reality, which is usually conditioned by middle-class ideology. Realism, then, is quite insidious because it just repeats back to the spectator what the common understanding of reality is.

Synge wrote his plays in a style that he liked to call 'transfigured realism'. He had borrowed this term from a comparative social scientist and philosopher, Herbert Spencer. Spencer's theory of transfigured realism argued that things are never quite as they seem. What Spencer meant by this is that reality is never completely objective, but neither is it entirely subjective, because reality is always shifting and changing. In his notebook, Synge recorded Spencer's theory:

> transfigured realism simply asserts objective existence as separate from and independent of subjective existence. But it asserts neither that any one mode of this existence is in reality that which it seems, nor that connexions among its modes are objectively what they seem.[10]

Synge's transfigured realism meant that *The Playboy* was grounded in social reality, but at the same time that reality was also enhanced and embellished for the purposes of art.

During the *Playboy* disturbances, the *Irish Times* received a letter from Ellen Duncan, the curator of Dublin's Municipal Gallery of Modern Art. Her letter hit the nail on the head: 'the battle between "The Playboy of the Western World" and the Abbey Theatre pit is the old battle between realism and the forces of reaction, with which we are already familiar in other forms of art.'[11] This is why *The Playboy* caused such a fuss, because those who caused disturbances knew that Synge was satirising Irish culture through his realistic depiction of Irish life. In the play Synge was making a joke out of what he understood to be the reality of life on the west coast of Ireland. But at the very same time he wasn't joking at all. He was being incredibly serious, as he himself pointed out: 'parts of it are, or are meant to be, extravagant comedy, still a great deal that is in it, and a great deal more that is behind it, is perfectly serious, when looked at in a certain light.'[12] That Synge's play was being perfectly serious was extremely problematic. Certain members of the audience had no other choice but to protest; there was no way that Synge could get away with contesting their dominant understanding of reality. Synge's uncomfortable truth was not welcome here. But what was that uncomfortable truth?

When the play was first performed Ireland was in a desperate struggle to achieve independence from the British Empire. The political struggle for national independence looked towards places such as County Mayo as the symbolic ideal of Ireland. The west of Ireland was supposedly untouched and uncorrupted by British ideology; it was certainly not envisioned as a place that celebrated patricide. But the uncomfortable truth was that large parts of the west of Ireland were in a horrible socio-economic condition after years of mismanagement. The worst-affected areas were officially called the Congested Districts: areas of land that were struck by poverty and starvation because of overpopulation. Synge visited the Congested Districts two years before *The Playboy* was performed, and he wrote a series of articles about the Districts for the *Manchester Guardian* (the predecessor to today's *Guardian* newspaper). In one article about life in Mayo he comments how 'the people [are] near to pauperism!'[13] In his final article for the newspaper he concluded that 'with renewed life in the country [and] many changes of the methods of government', life 'in the worst districts of Mayo' could be ameliorated.[14] In private Synge was absolutely appalled by what he saw, but he wrote a letter to his close friend Stephen MacKenna saying, 'I like not lifting the rags from my mother country for to tickle the sentiments of Manchester.'[15] Synge was not going to critique the mismanagement of the Congested Districts in Mayo too much because he wanted to defend Ireland from being wrongly stereotyped by the British public as a primitive country. Two years later, however, *The Playboy* revealed the reality of life in Mayo, as Synge understood it.

The political movement for national independence drew strength from the cultural movement and vice versa. By satirising the symbolic centre of cultural nationalism Synge was damaging the political movement. As I will go on to explain in the next chapter, the people who took the illusion of art far too faithfully were members of the Gaelic League and Sinn Féin, two organisations that supported Ireland's national independence from the British Empire. For Synge, nationalism in the theatre was pointless. All Synge really cared about was the importance of artistic expression. In order really to understand *The Playboy*'s uncomfortable truths we must first place the play in the context of the Ireland of Synge's time. The next chapter explores how Synge came to be a playwright, and what influenced him to write about the uncomfortable truths that *The Playboy* exposed.

Notes

1   *The Playboy of the Western World* was first performed on 26 January
    1907 in the Abbey Theatre, Dublin, by the Irish National Theatre
    Society. Cast: W. G. Fay (Christopher Mahon), Ambrose Power
    (Old Mahon), Arthur Sinclair (Michael James), Maire O'Neill
    (Pegeen Mike), F. J. Fay (Shawn Keogh), J. A. O'Rourke (Philly
    O'Cullen), J. M. Kerrigan (Jimmy Farrell), Sara Allgood (Widow
    Quin), Brigit O'Dempsey (Sara Tansey), Alice O'Sullivan (Susan
    Brady), Mary Craig (Honor Blake), and Harry Young and
    Udolphus Wright (peasants). It was first published by Maunsel
    (Dublin) in 1907.
2   *CW*, Vol. IV, 149.
3   Peter Crawley, 'A Decade Framed by Playboys', *Irish Times*, 2
    December 2009.
4   *CW*, Vol. IV, 169.
5   NLI MS 1805, Vol. I, 26 January 1907, fos. 63–64, and 31 January
    1907, fo. 74.
6   'Police In', *Irish Independent*, 29 January 1907.
7   'The Abbey Theatre', *The Freeman's Journal*, 31 January 1907.
8   'Police In.',
9   *CW*, Vol. IV, 53–54.
10 TCD MS 4379, fo. 85r.
11 Ellen Duncan, 'The Playboy', *Irish Times*, 29 January 1907.
12 J. M. Synge to the Editor of *Irish Times*, 30 January 1907, *CL*,
    Vol. I, 286.
13 *CW*, Vol. II, 330.
14 Ibid., 343.
15 J. M. Synge to Stephen MacKenna, 30 May 1905, *CL*, Vol. I,
    112.

Context

This chapter places *The Playboy* in context with Synge's life; his career as a playwright; and the social, economic and political situation in the Ireland of his time. In order really to get to the heart of the play and understand why it was so provocative, it is important to place the play in three key contexts: attitudes towards religion, class and culture in Synge's Ireland; Synge's life in Paris, the Aran Islands and County Mayo; and the importance of the Abbey Theatre. These three contexts will be explored individually but, in the first instance, it is important briefly to summarise Synge's short life.

Synge's life

In 1871 Synge was born in Rathfarnham, a suburb south of Dublin. He was the youngest of five children. His family were highly educated and comparably wealthy. His father practised as a lawyer, specialising in the conveyance of land, and his mother raised the children. Synge had a comparably conservative childhood that was plagued by frequent illness. In February 1889 he entered the University of Dublin,

Trinity College. He graduated in 1892. Soon after graduating from Trinity he moved to Germany to continue his studies in music. By 1895 Synge had given up his career of being a professional musician and he found himself in Paris taking postgraduate courses in French literature and comparative phonetics and, later, Irish and Homeric civilisation. Synge made a continual return to Paris for the next seven years. His life there runs in tandem with his life on the Aran Islands – three islands off the west coast of Ireland on which he found the ideas for four of his seven plays. Consequently, the impact of life in Paris and life in Aran on Synge's writing of *The Playboy* can hardly be overstated. Synge made his final trip to the Aran Islands in 1902, and his final trip to Paris in 1903.

In February 1905 Synge met actor Maire O'Neill, who went by her stage-name of Molly Allgood. Molly's sister was the actor Sara Allgood, a founding member of the Irish National Theatre Society, which went on to found the Abbey Theatre. The first three directors of the theatre were W. B. Yeats, Lady Augusta Gregory and Synge himself. In 1907 Molly performed the role of Pegeen Mike in *The Playboy*; the part was written for her. In October 1908, Mrs. Synge died, and just five months later, Synge lay dying of Hodgkin's disease. With tears in her eyes Molly begged the nurses to do something, anything. There was nothing they could do. The night before he died, Synge toasted a glass of champagne. He would not see the morning, and was buried alongside his mother in Mount Jerome Cemetery in south Dublin on 26 March 1909.

Religion, class and culture

In Synge's Ireland there was one dominant class: the Catholic middle class. The Catholic middle class had risen to social, economic and political power across a seventy-year period and now, at the dawn of the twentieth century, this class controlled professional and public life. Achieving such social, economic and political power had not been easy. Up until 1829 Irish Catholics were subjected to penal laws that had been put in place in 1607. The penal laws were designed to strengthen Protestant culture in Ireland. In so doing, apartheid was created whereby the Irish Catholic was denied basic human rights. Catholics were not allowed to enter public office and they were fined for not attending Protestant church services. The subjugation of Catholic Ireland meant that from the beginning of the seventeenth century, Protestant Ireland ascended to social, economic and political dominance. This class was known as the Anglo-Irish Ascendancy. Synge was born into it, and in order really to understand *The Playboy* it is important to understand the heritage of the Anglo-Irish Ascendancy.

In 1603 James VI of Scotland united the kingdoms of England and Scotland with Ireland under personal union, receiving the title of James I. A personal union is a one where one monarch rules over two or more countries, but each individual country has its own distinct laws, territorial boundaries and system of governance. James I was a Protestant king who was almost assassinated by the Catholic Gunpowder Plot in 1605. With Catholic Ireland subjected to penal laws, King James I decided to tighten his grip on Ireland by resettling Scottish and English nobility to the province of Ulster in what came to be known as the Plantation of Ulster. Catholic rebellions were numerous but largely unsuccessful, and as the years rolled by the penal laws became increasingly harsh. The Plantation of Ulster marks the beginning of the Anglo-Irish Ascendancy.

Even though the Ascendancy were a relatively small demographic, they were the dominant class in Ireland throughout the eighteenth century. To be a member of the Ascendancy in eighteenth-century Ireland had nothing to do with being a descendant from a noble or military family, but everything to do with the Ascendancy's attachment to Anglicanism: the Church of England. Since the sixteenth century the Church of England had been in communion with the Church of Ireland. Anglicanism provided the Ascendancy with a refined English sense of culture and style that had the surface appearance of being aristocratic.

Synge's family had moved from England to Ireland in the seventeenth century. By the time Synge was born, the Ascendancy had lost its aristocratic aura, but still thought that it belonged to a higher class than the Catholic middle classes. For example, Mrs. Synge was afraid that the family 'would not be free from fleas' upon realising that a Catholic family owned their rented holiday accommodation in County Wicklow in the summer of 1895.[1] Synge, however, had a complicated relationship to the Ascendancy and he was keen to foreground his Irish background as opposed to his English background. In a letter to a German translator of his works Synge introduced himself:

> my Christian names are John Millington, my family were originally called Millington, and Queen Elizabeth is said to have changed this name to 'Synge' they sang so finely. Synge is, of course, pronounced 'sing', since then they have been in Ireland for nearly three centuries, so that there is now a good deal of Celtic, or more exactly, Gaelic blood in the family.[2]

However, by the beginning of the nineteenth century the Ascendancy began a slow decline in power. In 1801 the Act of Union came into effect, which removed the personal union between Ireland and England, and the United Kingdom was formally established. Parliament in Westminster, London, now governed Ireland, which meant that the Ascendancy no longer had administrative governance of Ireland. Some members of the Ascendancy returned to England. Those who remained were left in an awkward, if ironic, position. The Anglo-Irish Ascendancy wanted to forget their attachment to England and yet, at the same time, they wanted to hold on to their elevated social status. By 1829 the penal laws were abolished and a liberal attitude towards governance in Ireland was being established. In 1845 the Great Famine decimated Catholic Ireland, leaving vast expanses of land completely barren. What emerged from the Famine was a generation of Catholic farmers who had large farms, known as 'strong farmers' because of the strength of their socio-economic position. Money from farming flowed through the country as Catholic middle classes entered professional and public life, but what really defined the Catholic middle classes in Synge's Ireland was the orthodoxy of Roman Catholicism. From 1850 to 1875 the Irish devotional revolution changed Irish society by enforcing strict codes of religious and social conduct. The archbishop of Dublin, Cardinal Paul Cullen, managed the Devotional Revolution, and he neatly summarised the rapid rise of Catholic Ireland: 'We are the Catholic population of the United Kingdom. A population growing every day in wealth and social importance.'[3]

The majority of middle-class Catholic Ireland now had its sights firmly set on achieving national independence from the British Empire. The political party that campaigned for national independence was Sinn Féin, founded by Arthur Griffith in 1905. 'We are firm believers in the freedom of art', wrote Griffith, but any artist associated with a National Society should 'pay the price by relinquishing some of that freedom'.[4] The art that Sinn Féin wanted to see was thinly disguised propaganda for cultural nationalism. Sinn Féin were supported in their campaign for artistic propaganda by the Gaelic League, founded by Douglas Hyde and Eoin MacNeill in 1893. In 1892 Hyde gave a famous lecture entitled 'The Necessity for De-Anglicising Ireland' to the Irish National Literary Society, in which he argued that the Irish language should be preserved and promoted. A year later the League was founded as a means to support cultural nationalism. In 1901 Hyde presented his culturally nationalist play written in Irish: *Casadh an tSugáin* (*The Twisting of the Rope*). Performed by members of the League, the play is almost the complete inverse of *The Playboy*: a community in the west of Ireland expels a stranger named Hanrahan to ensure that the young woman (Oona) whom he is attempting to seduce remains with her fiancé (Sheamus). It is little wonder, then, that the League harshly critiqued *The Playboy* in their own newspaper *An Claidheamh Soluis* (*The Sword of Light*): '[Synge] is using the stage for the propagation of a monstrous gospel of animalism, or revolt against sane and sweet ideals, of bitter contempt for all that is fine and worthy, not merely in Christian morality, but in human nature itself.'[5] Furthermore, the fact that the play was written by an Anglo-Irishman was not lost on either the League or Sinn Féin. The problem, then, with religion and class in Synge's Ireland was that it influenced the definition and reception of Irish culture and politics and, ultimately, the reception of *The Playboy*. The play was considered to be highly offensive towards the Gaelic League's cultural support for Sinn Féin's bid for national independence. However, in 1928 Synge's good friend Stephen MacKenna wrote that while Synge 'refused to support the Gaelic League' because of the 'lying that gathered around the political movement', he would still 'die for the theory that Synge was most intensely Nationalist; he habitually spoke with rage and bitter baleful eyes, of the English in Ireland, though he was proud of his own remote Englishry'.[6] *The Playboy* may have affected the bid for national independence but ultimately the pain that it caused went much deeper than nationalism; Synge's satire was carefully aimed at the social practices of middle-class Catholic Ireland.

The Playboy satirises both the stereotype of the middle-class Irish Catholic and the middle-class Irish Catholic's appreciation of Irish culture. In performance, attitudes towards Ascendancy and Catholic religion, class and culture met head on. After *The Playboy* was first performed Synge wrote a letter to MacKenna saying that

> the scurrility, and ignorance and treachery of some of the attacks upon me have rather disgusted me with the middle class Irish Catholic. As you know I have the wildest admiration for the Irish Peasants, and for Irish men of known or unknown genius – do you bow? – but between the two there's an ungodly ruck of fat-faced, sweaty-headed, swine. They are in Dublin, and Kingstown, and alas in all country towns – they stink of porter . . . Irish humour is dead, MacKenna, and I've got influenza.[7]

Synge's basic point is that he should be able to satirise Catholic middle-class life freely, but the Catholic middle classes did not appreciate such satire from an Anglo-Irish playwright. As the next chapter will demonstrate, *The Playboy* provides a snapshot of religion, culture and class in Ireland at the turn of the twentieth century. However, before we consider the play in further detail it is important to consider how Synge's time in Paris and on the Aran Islands directly influenced how he wrote the play.

Paris

After spending eighteen months studying music in Germany, Synge arrived in Paris on New Year's Day 1895. Staying in hotels and rented accommodation in and around the Parisian Quarter on the Left Bank, Synge lived a bohemian lifestyle, maintaining that Paris offered him 'a breath of the wickedness'.[8]

In Paris Synge began studying comparative phonetics, French literature, medieval literature and Irish and Homeric civilisation. All four subjects can be identified in the play. He studied comparative phonetics – the comparison of the sounds of different languages – at the École Pratique des Hautes Études (Practical School of Higher Studies). Synge learnt about patois – the importance of dialect and vernacular – and his studies in this subject area would influence how he crafted the dialect used in *The Playboy*: Hiberno-English, a blending of the Irish and English language. Just how Synge did this will be fully explored in the next chapter, but for now it is important to point out that one of the reasons he was able to do this was because he had a strong academic foundation in the subject.

Synge studied medieval and French literature at the Université de Paris - Sorbonne. It was here that he encountered the work of François Rabelais and Molière. Rabelais was a medieval French writer who satirised Renaissance humanism. The whole point of Renaissance humanism was the desire to use newly discovered classical texts from ancient Greece and Rome to change European humanity; there was much to be learnt from the works of Plato, Aristotle and Seneca, for example. Rabelais satirised the thought that every man and woman had the potential to be scholarly and civilised. His influence on comic writing was so important that the adjective 'Rabelaisian' is used to describe colloquial humour and the kind of intimate, indecent jokes that one might share in private. What Synge learnt from reading Rabelais was the importance of satire to bring polite society back down to earth through impolite language. The next chapter will give specific examples of Rabelais's influence on the play.

Born Jean-Baptiste Poquelin, Molière made a career in the theatre from satirising the social customs and manners of French high society. What Synge learnt from reading Molière's plays was the importance of comic structure and using stereotypes when writing a farce. In Molière's plays the jokes are carefully structured so that they come thick and fast. In so doing, they push each scene, and therefore each act, towards a farcical climax where the stakes are very high. The next chapter will give specific examples of Molière's influence on the play.

Synge also studied Irish and Homeric civilisation at the Sorbonne. What he learnt here was the importance of really understanding the society and culture of Celtic Ireland. Much of the cultural nationalism that supported Ireland's bid for national independence invoked false concepts and stereotypes of Celtic Ireland – considered to be a mystical land of poetry and culture – and the example of what Ireland could be if the British were to leave. Synge's studies at the Sorbonne put an end to that myth. He learnt that Celtic Ireland was a violent, sexual society, just like the community in *The Playboy*. Consequently, when Synge began writing plays for the Abbey Theatre he would seek to dispel the myth of this mystical, magical utopia. It did not matter to Synge that his play offended the dream of Celtic Ireland because he felt vindicated by his studies at the Sorbonne.

In many respects Paris provided Synge with an excellent foundation to begin writing *The Playboy*: the importance of satire, the importance of stereotype and dramatic structure, and the importance of telling the truth about the Celtic dream of Ireland. All he needed now was a good story, and he would find it on the Aran Islands.

The Aran Islands and County Mayo

The three Aran Islands lie off the coast of Galway. Inis Mór (Big Island) is considerably larger than the two smaller islands: Inis Meáin (Middle Island) and Inis Oírr (East Island). Synge first visited Aran (a collective noun for all three islands) in May 1898, and he continuously returned to the islands for the next four years, choosing to spend the majority of his time on Inis Meáin.

On Inis Meáin Synge encountered 'an old man, the oldest on the island', who told him 'anecdotes – not folk-tales – of things that have happened here in his lifetime'.[9] This storyteller is commonly believed to be a man named Pat Dirane, whom Synge frequently refers to in his book about life on Aran: *The Aran Islands*. However, there is no evidence to suggest this is the case. In fact, Synge had every reason to conceal this storyteller's identity because the anecdote that he told

Synge actually occurred and, furthermore, it broke the law. This is how Synge recalled the story:

> He often tells me about a Connaught man who killed his father with the blow of a spade when he was in a passion, and then fled to this island and threw himself on the mercy of some of the natives with whom he was said to be related. They hid him in a hole – which the old man has shown me – and kept him safe for weeks, though the police came and searched for him, and he could hear their boots grinding over his head. In spite of a reward which was offered, the island was incorruptible, and after much trouble the man was safely shipped to America.[10]

This is the true story of man named William Mally from Callow, County Galway, who attacked his 'quiet and elderly father', Pat Mally, in January 1873. As the *Galway Express* reported at the time, William 'was preparing a little paddock (not larger than an ordinary room in size) for early potatoes; [Pat] went out to prevent him, when a scuffle ensued; the son lifted his spade and struck his father with it; he fell insensible'.[11] Next, William brought his father into the house and presented the deceased parent to his step-mother, before running into the mountains. For several nights Mally sheltered from the falling snow in bushes, ditches and caves before boarding a boat to the Aran Islands from Carraroe, County Galway. Mally arrived on Inis Mór, but when the police received word that he was hiding there he fled to Inis Meáin, which is where Synge first heard the story. The police followed Mally to Inis Meáin but they could not find him, and he eventually escaped on a boat carrying potatoes to Tralee, County Kerry. From there he fled to America to be later joined by his wife. According to Aran folklore, Mally was nicknamed 'the playboy' because the islanders threw many parties for him in an attempt to try and appease his remorse for killing his father. Synge took this story as one of the inspirations for *The Playboy*. The other inspiration was the case of James Lynchehaun, which made national headlines.

Lynchehaun was a tenant on an estate on 'the most remote spot on the remote island of Achill' in County Mayo, which belonged to an English woman, Agnes MacDonnell, known locally as the 'Yellow Lady' because of her wealthy social status.[12] In 1894 a disagreement between MacDonnell and Lynchehaun over rent resulted in Lynchehaun setting fire to MacDonnell's house and beating her to within an inch of her life. Reporting from the scene, the *Irish Times* accounts for how MacDonnell was

> brutally maltreated while endeavouring to escape from the flames. Her skull was fractured. Her nose completely torn from her face, and her hair which was plaited and fastened to the crown of her head, forcibly pulled off, taking with it jagged portions of her scalp. She lies in the most precarious condition, and there is little hope of her surviving the shocking injuries she sustained. [13]

This is why one of the village girls (Susan Brady) in the play refers to the Lynchehaun case when trying to figure out what 'crime' Christy has committed:

> maybe he's stolen off to Belmullet with the boots of Michael James, and you'd have a right so to follow after him, Sara Tansey, and you the one yoked the ass cart and

drove ten miles to set your eye on the man bit the yellow lady's nostril on the northern shore.[14]

The police eventually arrested Lynchehaun and MacDonnell survived. Even after all she had been through, she still referred to Lynchehaun as a 'fine, young, strong, dark, animal-looking man'.[15] As Lynchehaun was being transported to prison he escaped and went on the run for a further three months. He was later captured and spent seven years in Maryborough prison in County Laoise. Lynchehaun escaped prison in 1903 and fled to the United States of America (Indianapolis) where he was later captured. However, he was not extradited to Ireland because in 1904 a judge in America considered his attack on MacDonnell to be politically motivated, as she was an English woman living in colonial Ireland. Lynchehuan's case was famous in Synge's Ireland for its horrific violence, sexual subtext and peculiar take on social justice. *The Playboy* draws extensively on these themes; even in Synge's drafts of the play characters discuss how Christy won't be caught by the police, because 'they never touched Lynchehaun when they knew the kind he was'.[16] Clearly, in Synge's mind, Christy and the Lynchehaun case were not very far removed.

When *The Playboy* disturbances began, Synge said it did 'not matter a rap' what critics thought he based the play on, and he insisted: 'I wrote the play because it pleased me, and it just happens that I know Irish life the best, so I made my methods Irish.'[17] But Synge was not being entirely honest. In a private letter to Stephen MacKenna he admitted:

It isn't quite accurate to say, I think, that the thing is a generalization from a single case. *If* the idea had occurred to me I could and would just as readily written the thing [*sic*], as it stands, without the Lynchehaun case or the Aran case. The story – in its <u>ESSENCE</u> – is probable, given the psychic state of the locality. I used the cases afterwards to controvert the critics who said it was *impossible*. Amen.[18]

The cases of Mally and Lynchehaun influenced the structure of the play, and also provided Synge with the idea of how to write the part of Christy Mahon. Much of the comedy in Christy comes from the fact that his character does not conform to the stereotype of a man that could commit the crimes that Mally and Lynchehaun committed. All Synge needed now was a theatre in which to stage the play.

The Abbey Theatre

In 1897 Yeats, Lady Gregory and Edward Martyn (another Ascendancy playwright) published a manifesto entitled the 'Manifesto for the Irish Literary Theatre', which stated:

We propose to have performed in Dublin, in the spring of every year certain Celtic and Irish plays . . . We hope to find in Ireland an uncorrupted and imaginative audience trained to listen by its passion for oratory, and believe that our desire to bring upon the stage the deeper thoughts and emotions of Ireland will ensure for us a tolerant welcome . . . We will show that Ireland is not the home of buffoonery and of easy sentiment, as it has been represented, but the home of ancient idealism. We are confident of the support of the Irish people, who are weary of misrepresentation, in carrying out a work that is outside all the political questions that divide us.[19]

The Irish Literary Theatre did exactly what their manifesto stated they would do, and in 1899 they began to perform plays in small halls in Dublin. These plays, however, were quite unlike anything the Irish theatregoer had seen before. Before this point the dominant forms of theatre in Dublin were melodrama and the musical. These forms are very much dependent on using stereotypes in drawing the spectator into 'easy sentiment', and the Irish Literary Theatre changed all that by creating poetical plays about Ireland that would have been considered high art at the time. In his Nobel Prize for Literature acceptance speech Yeats remarked:

> the theatres of Dublin had nothing about them we could call our own. They were empty buildings hired by English travelling companies, and we wanted Irish plays and Irish players. When we thought of these plays we thought of everything that was romantic and poetical, because the nationalism we had called – the nationalism every generation had called up in moments of discouragement – was romantic and poetical. . . . Two events brought us victory: a friend gave us a theatre, and we found a strange man of genius, John Synge.[20]

In 1902 brothers William George Fay and Francis John Fay created the Irish Dramatic Company. The Fay brothers trained amateur actors, and in 1903 the Irish Literary Theatre joined forces with the Fay brothers to create the Irish National Theatre Society, with Synge as one of its founding members. Yeats secured financial assistance (£1,300) from his friend Annie Horniman, an English tea heiress, and with that money a Dublin architect, Joseph Holloway, renovated an old Mechanics Theatre in Dublin as the Abbey Theatre.

By virtue of the fact that the Abbey Theatre was the home of the *Irish National* Theatre Society, the plays that were performed there were confused with cultural nationalism. Matters were made worse because the dominant form of theatrical representation during the Abbey's formative years came to be known as 'cottage kitchen realism', as plays were invariably set in cottage kitchens and rated on their 'peasant quality' – that is, their ability 'faithfully' to represent the socio-economic conditions of the peasantry. The peasantry in the west of Ireland was considered to be symbolic of an Ireland that had not been tainted by British rule. In fact, the peasantry in the west of Ireland was one of the poorest socio-economic classes in western Europe, hence the need for the Congested Districts. Performances at the Abbey Theatre romanticised these harsh realities. In so doing, performances were inextricably linked to cultural nationalism in both form (cottage kitchen realism) and content (peasant quality). This is one of the reasons that Sinn Féin and the Gaelic League were attracted to attending performances at the Abbey. However, what they saw in *The Playboy* was, from their perspective, not attractive at all. *The Playboy* dramatised buffoonery and easy sentiment, as well as drunkenness, stupidity and violence. 'Nationality is the breath of art', maintained Sinn Féin, and furthermore, the 'assurance that a Theatre intended to be a free and National Theatre has no propaganda save that of good art – savours to us of consideration of the Englishmen who are among us'.[21] The position of the Gaelic League and Sinn Féin was simple: plays performed by the Irish National Theatre Society should not critique Ireland. *The Playboy* did just that.

In many respects the Abbey Theatre during Synge's career was much more than a theatre. It was an arena that staged contests between differing attitudes to religion, class and culture in Ireland. That *The Playboy* had been influenced by Synge's studies in Paris, and the cases of Mally and Lynchehaun did not matter to those who caused the disturbances. Just how the disturbances unfolded will be explored in due course. However, before the first performances of the play are explored, it is necessary to examine the play in detail in order to understand why it was so offensive.

Notes

1 TCD SSMS 6191, fo. 1022.
2 J. M. Synge to Max Meyerfeld, 12 September 1905, NLI MS 778, fo. 13r–v.
3 Cardinal Paul Cullen, quoted in Emmet Larkin, *The Making of the Roman Catholic Church in Ireland: 1850–1860* (Chapel Hill, NC: University of North California Press, 1980), 447.
4 Arthur Griffith, 'All Ireland', *United Irishman*, 17 October 1903.
5 P. H. Pearse, 'The Passing of Anglo-Irish Drama', *An Claidheamh Soluis*, 9 February 1907.
6 Stephen MacKenna, 'Synge', *Irish Statesman*, 3 November 1928.
7 J. M. Synge to Stephen MacKenna, 9 April 1907, *CL*, Vol. I, 330.
8 J. M. Synge to Stephen MacKenna, n.d., *CL*, Vol. I, 41.
9 *CW*, Vol. II, 95.
10 Ibid.
11 'Awful Murder of a Father by His Own Son', *Galway Express*, 1 February 1873.
12 'A Terrible Outrage on Achill Island', *Irish Times*, 6 October 1894.
13 Ibid.
14 *CW*, Vol. IV, 97.
15 Mrs. MacDonnell, quoted in James Carney, *The Playboy and The Yellow Lady* (Dublin: Poolbeg, 1986), 5.
16 *CW*, Vol. IV, 311.
17 J. M. Synge, quoted in A. F., 'I Don't Care a Rap', *Dublin Evening Mail*, 29 January 1907.

18 J. M. Synge to Stephen MacKenna, 17 April 1907, *CL*, Vol. I, 333. Emphasis in original.
19 Lady Augusta Gregory, *Our Irish Theatre* (New York: Capricorn, 1965), 8–9.
20 W. B. Yeats, *Autobiographies* (London: Macmillan, 1955), 560, 566.
21 Griffith, 'All Ireland'.

2

Play

Synge began writing *The Playboy* in 1904. He finished it in 1906, but would make minor edits to the play in January 1907 during rehearsals. This chapter offers a detailed textual analysis of the play. Much of its power comes from Synge's emphasis on language to captivate, persuade and influence people; Christy Mahon is only transformed into the playboy of the western world through believing his own 'mighty talk'.[1] But for many members of Synge's original audience, the talk in the play was far *too* mighty. Joseph Holloway, the architect of the Abbey Theatre, wrote in his diary that the play was 'wallowing in filthy expression, & beastly character'.[2] The central concern of this chapter is to analyse the language that Synge used to write *The Playboy*, and I will explore it from four key perspectives: dialect, comic structure, religion and class and gender and sexuality.

Dialect

The language of *The Playboy* can be difficult to read and/or hear for the first time. For example, the *Guardian*'s review of a 2011 performance at London's Old Vic Theatre pointed out that 'almost everyone has quibbles with the language', and concluded that 'the bits we could understand were good'.[3] The so-called problem lies in Synge's writing in a dialect known as Hiberno-English, which is a blend between the Irish and English languages. Hiberno-English was spoken by a large demographic of rural Ireland when Synge was alive as the island began to learn to speak English. As native Irish speakers learnt the new language, they naturally translated English back into Irish so that the foreign language could be understood. In so doing, native Irish speakers spoke English words but with the syntax of the Irish language.

Let me give some examples of how Synge used Irish syntax to write *The Playboy* in Hiberno-English. Widow Quin says 'I'm after meeting Shawn Keogh'.[4] In Irish that phrase translates as: 'tá mé tar éis castáil le Shawn Keogh', literally 'I after meeting Shawn Keogh'. The Irish language is a very descriptive, personal language and the syntax is important in this example. If the Widow Quin were to say 'I met Shawn Keogh' then the equvialent in Irish, 'Chas mé le Shawn Keogh', would not indicate *how long ago* Shawn Keogh was met. By including 'after meeting', 'tá mé tar éis castáil', the Irish language accounts for the fact that Shawn has just been met very recently. Let me give another example. Michael James says to Christy: 'is it yourself is fearing the polis?'.[5] In Irish this phrase transaltes as 'an bhfuil faitíos ort fhéin roimh na poilíní?': literally 'is it fear you yourself before the police?'. The Irish language emphasises the self, and this phrase lays emphasis on how Christy *feels*, as well as what is causing him to feel this way. The Hiberno-English dialect in the play might seem tricky to read and/or hear for the first time, but the sheer lyricism and poetical nature of the dialect allowed Synge to play with language to create beautiful, absurd and grotesque images. Synge knew that some of his playing with language had the potential to offend, and so he decided to write a public disclaimer: 'in writing *The Playboy of the Western World*', Synge maintained, 'I have used one or two words only, that I have not heard amongst the country people of Ireland'.[6] Synge believed that it was important to foreground 'the imagination of the people, and the language they use' because 'on the stage one must have reality, and one must have joy'.[7] Synge's notebooks reveal that much of the coarse dialogue was overheard in West Kerry: for Synge, reality was the foundation of all joy on the stage.

In 1903 Synge decided to visit Mountain Stage, West Kerry. Significantly, this is why Christy is from Kerry. Synge recorded a story told to him about an old woman who married a young man. The old woman was thought to be rich, but when she died it transpired that she was not rich at all. The person telling the story to Synge uses the phrase 'hoping [for the money] sooner or later in the form of hog, dog, or devil'.[8] This phrase makes its way into *The Playboy* when Christy says he left his father's house and has been 'walking forward facing hog, dog, or divil on the highway of the road'.[9] Other references that Synge recorded in Kerry include 'mule kicking the stars',[10] which finds its way into Old Mahon's description of Christy's mule during the beach races: 'look at the mule he has kicking the stars'.[11] From another source Synge recorded the phrase 'it'd make the green stones cry to think of it'.[12] Pegeen Mike uses this phrase to remind Christy that if the police were to catch him, there would be no telling what 'thing they'd do, if it'd make the green stones cry itself to think of you swaying and swiggling at the butt of a rope'.[13] Another source in his Kerry notebook uses the phrase 'as naked as an ash tree in the moon of March'.[14] Christy uses this phrase to characterise his father's drunken lifestyle, where Old Mahon wakes up and enters 'the yard as naked as an ash tree in the moon of May'.[15] Synge recorded a conversation in which a 'man hangs his dog and you heard it screeching half the day and it hanging from the head of a ditch',[16] and 'Daneen Sullivan Kenmare wipes out all other tinkers – a great warrant to tell stories'.[17] Both of these phrases, overheard in West Kerry, find their way into the play. Pegeen compares Christy's 'crime' to 'the way Jimmy Farrell hanged his dog from the licence and had it screeching and wriggling three hours at the butt of a string'.[18] She also references 'Daneen Sullivan', who 'got six months for maiming ewes, and he a great warrant to tell stories'.[19]

'Anyone who has lived in real intimacy with the Irish peasant will know that the wildest sayings and ideas in this play are tame indeed',[20] claimed a very nervous Synge on the eve of the first performance. That Synge maintained he had actually heard these phrases is very important because it allowed him to ground his language in a degree of social truth, which is the very foundation of satire. In order to understand how the play is a satire, it is important to understand its comic structure.

The comic structure of the play

The Playboy is a comic masterpiece of modern theatre because of its intricate comic structure, and an indulgent, playful relationship with language is the foundation of this structure. Overall, the play is a satire, but it also contains a lot of farcical situations. Before I approach it in terms of its two key themes of class and religion and gender and sexuality, let me first explain how comic reversals, farce and caricature contribute to satire in the play.

Comic reversals

A comic reversal is when the unexpected happens with humorous results. *The Playboy* is full of comic reversals; Old Mahon's sudden entrance at the climax of the play is a good example. Up until this point in the play Christy is the playboy of the western world, but the second his 'deceased' father enters the community everything is reversed. What makes comic reversals particularly effective is their ability to bring events crashing back down to earth. Some of the comic reversals in *The Playboy* are particularly effective because they are ironic. For irony to be particularly humorous it has to be an especially cold, unsentimental reading of an event. We often find irony humorous because it is the absolute opposite reading to what is expected, and the play's biggest joke is an excellent example of an ironic comic reversal: Old Mahon was supposed to be dead, but he has walked right into the middle of the community to punish his son.

Synge rejected anyone who wanted to 'exalt the Irish peasant into a type of almost virtue, frugal, self-sacrificing, valiant, and I know not what',[21] because he quite correctly thought that this was an absolute myth: 'though the Irish peasant has many beautiful virtues, it is idle to assert that he is totally unacquainted with the deadly sins, and many minor rogueries'.[22] The problem with *The Playboy* was that Synge's peasant, Christy Mahon, has committed a crime that far exceeds a minor roguery: patricide. Synge establishes Christy's attempted murder of his father by allowing the Mayo community to indicate many other crimes that Christy could be running away from: stealing, polygamy, sexual harassment and grievous bodily harm, even fighting for the British army. This technique of listing all the other crimes that Christy could have committed means that his attempted murder of his father is given dramatic emphasis and, significantly, it allows Synge to set up an ironic comic reversal. Placing dramatic emphasis on Christy's violent act invites the reader/spectator into being complicit with the Mayo community in defining Christy as 'a daring fellow',[23] because just like the Mayo community we also think that if Christy hasn't committed any 'deadly sins [or] many minor rogueries',[24] then just *what* has he done? Next, Synge uses a comic reversal to great effect: we are faced with a seemingly brave character capable of committing violent acts, and yet Christy appears as '*a slight young man . . . very tired and frightened and dirty*'.[25] And then Christy makes his big admission: 'I killed my poor father, Tuesday was a week, for doing the like of that.'[26] Pegeen reacts the quickest – '[*with blank amazement*]. Is it killed your father?'[27] – but her blank amazement is the only indication of the community's horror. Synge's point is quite clear: patricide is a lesser crime than all of the others listed. This is an ironic comic reversal in full effect, because instead of running for the police, the community is far more interested in the drama of Christy's patricide, wanting to know how the dirty deed played out. Michael James asks if Christy used 'a hilted knife' and Pegeen asks if he 'shot him dead'.[28] Christy is only too happy to indulge the community in the theatricality of his crime: 'I just riz the loy and let fall the edge of it on the ridge of his skull, and he went down at my feet like an empty sack, and never let a grunt or groan from him at all.'[29]

Synge uses this violent crime as a continual comic reversal throughout the play, and each time Christy tells his story to new people he meets it becomes more and more dramatic, allowing him to extend the irony of the comic reversal. For example, the next time Christy tells his story to the village girls it is considerably longer and full of drama. Christy recalls how he 'turned around with my back to the north, and I hit a blow on the ridge of his skull, laid him stretched out, and he split to the knob of his gullet'.[30] Instead of being shocked and appalled the village girls offer another ironic comic reversal: they simply say 'that's a grand story' and 'he tells it lovely'.[31] Comic reversals, and especially ones that are ironic, are solely used by Synge to increase the humour in his play. As I will demonstrate in my analysis of the two major themes of the play below, not everyone found Synge's ironic comic reversals to be humorous because they only supported satire and farce.

Farce

Farce places everyday people in absurd situations with humorous consequences. What makes farce so effective is when there is something at stake. When something is at stake, we sit back and watch stereotypical characters desperately try and keep control of things that they have no control over, knowing that if things go wrong then the whole illusion of control will come crashing down.

Synge believed that 'all decadence is opposed to true humour'.[32] Elements of farce are so essential to *The Playboy* because they offer light relief to the decadent language that Synge uses throughout the play. This is why Synge originally titled the play *The Murderer (a Farce)*.[33] Farce also allows Synge further to foreground the major theme of the play: the problems in believing in illusions. Characters in the play identify with elaborate language to create an illusory reality but, sooner or later, the real world will bring everyone and everything crashing back down to earth. As stated in the previous chapter, Synge's understanding of farce was very much dependent on his reading of Molière.

The vast majority of characters in Molière's plays are stereotypes. By dramatising simplified, socially classed characters, Molière is able to ridicule society's understanding of class, and Synge does the same. Synge's notebooks reveal that he wrote the moment when Shawn Keogh attempts to leave the shebeen as Christy arrives as a 'Molièrean climax of farce'.[34] I will go on to explain how Shawn embodies, for Synge, the pathetic Catholic middle-class stereotype, but for now let me explain how Synge uses farce to ridicule Shawn's social class. Shawn does not want to be left alone with his fiancé, Pegeen Mike, overnight in the shebeen because he is 'afeard of Father Reilly'.[35] So, he tries to escape the shebeen before Michael James and his friends leave. As Shawn tries to leave, Michael James catches him by the coat. Shawn screams, 'leave me go, Michael James, leave me go, you old Pagan, leave me go or I'll get the curse of the priests on you, and of the scarlet-coated bishops of the courts of Rome';[36] he wriggles out of his coat, which Michael James is holding, and runs out of the door. This moment is a Molièrean climax of farce because the stereotype of the completely in-control Catholic middle-class man has been brought crashing back down to earth. Molière's farces are intricately structured; characters know something that other characters don't and, in this way, comic irony is an important structural feature of his plays. The necessity of high stakes is also important because characters do not want other characters to find out their secrets. In many respects, the characters in Molière's plays have no control over events that are happening to them, and this is important because they are stereotypes. Therefore, if his characters are to change, to learn or to grow in any way, then the structure of the play has to have an impact on them, rather than the character changing the structure of the play. More often than not this is through Molière introducing a character or an event when characters least expect it, and Synge does the same in *The Playboy* when Old Mahon arrives.

When Old Mahon arrives in the community the stakes are immediately raised because Christy cannot let the illusion come crashing back down to earth. Significantly, Widow Quin is made aware that Old Mahon is Christy's father: now a character knows something others don't. She tries to persuade Old Mahon to leave because Christy has promised her that if she is successful in doing so he'll reward her with 'a mountainy ram, and a load of dung at Michaelmas'.[37] Synge, however, writes the play so that characters are forced to confront the cold reality that Christy has been telling lies. This is what Synge took from Molière: the narrative impacting on character, as opposed to the character changing the narrative. Essentially, Synge manipulates the plot to trap Christy. Of course, Christy attempts to change the narrative and, as he desperately tries to keep things under control, the comedy begins to build into a farce.

A key element of farce is that it should operate at a quick pace, and Synge switches elaborate language for short, simplified lines: 'I'll not leave Pegeen Mike.'[38] But he also honours the quick pace with physical comedy, another key element of farce: Christy is pulled this way and that, he squirms on the floor and he bites Shawn's leg. At the very climax of the farce, Old Mahon arrives to save Christy from being tortured and turned over to the police. This marks the end of the farce: everything has been brought back down to earth and normal order has resumed. Usually, at the end of farces, the stereotypical characters have learnt from the drama they have lived through, and Synge allows a brief moment of reflection. Christy is 'the master of all fights from now', whereas Pegeen has 'lost the only playboy of the western world'.[39] This is a typical farcical ending. In all farce there is a thin line between comedy and tragedy, and typically there is usually at least one character that is left feeling desperately upset, precisely because the high stakes have been lost. Synge ends the play in this way to allow us to reflect on an important point in both farce and satire: the joke is always at someone's expense. Farcical moments in *The Playboy* increase the effect of satire in the play because stereotypes are deconstructed, and we are asked to confront the cold reality of what happens when all the laughter stops. In his notebook Synge reflected quite deeply on the power of comedy, concluding that 'humour is the test of morals'.[40] For Synge, humour should make us reconsider the coordinates of our moral compass; he wants us to use humour to make us think about what is right and what is wrong.

Caricature

Caricature is exaggerating characteristics of people or places in a grotesque fashion for humorous results. *The Playboy* is full of caricature because a lot of the humour in the play is grotesque. Synge despised drama that presented 'the reality of life in joyless and pallid words'.[41] Accordingly, for Synge, 'in a good play every speech should be fully flavoured as a nut or apple'[42] and, furthermore, 'we should not go to the theatre as we go to a chemist's, or a dram-shop, but as we go to a dinner, where the good we need is taken with pleasure and excitement'.[43] Throughout the play Synge uses language to create absurd images. He then proceeds to clash these images to create caricatures of people or places. Let me give an example of caricature in the play: Old Mahon says that Christy used to come home from school 'with his legs lamed under him, and he blackened with his beatings like a tinker's ass'.[44] All of a sudden we are presented with a grotesque caricature of a badly bruised Christy and a tinker's ass. In this way, Synge uses caricature repeatedly to create larger-than-life characters. He does the same for place. For example, in order to emphasise the remoteness of the Mayo community that lies on 'the scruff of the hill',[45] Synge allows his characters to repeat how their surroundings are a 'dark [and] lonesome place'.[46] But Synge caricatures this. Pegeen is afraid of 'the dogs barking, and the calves mooing, and my own teeth rattling with the fear' because everyone and everything in this place is sinful; even the cows are described as 'breathing and sighing like Christian sinners in the white light of the moon', a phrase that Synge overheard in County Mayo.[47]

All this grotesque caricature didn't go down well, at all, with the vast majority of Synge's audience. The *Freeman's Journal* put the situation quite plainly:

> a strong protest must, however, be entered against this unmitigated, protracted libel upon Irish peasant men and, worse still, upon Irish peasant girlhood. The blood boils with indignation as one recalls the incidents, expressions, ideas of this squalid, offensive production, incongruously styled a comedy in three acts.[48]

By continually indulging in such rich language, Synge's own writing of the play can be seen as a self-reflexive commentary on Christy's playing with language to blur the boundaries between illusion and reality. But much more than this, Synge's playful relationship with language in the play summons many grotesque, crude and far-fetched caricatures, all of which are used not only to increase the humour in the play but also to cause maximum offence. And the moment in the play that caused the most offence came at the very end of Act III, when Christy is revealed as a liar.

We should remember that throughout the play Christy's violent story is only retold. Such reporting of violence is commonplace in theatre, and it can be traced back to ancient Greek theatre. However, for Synge, it was not enough that violence should be reported: it had to be shown. When Christy's father arrives in the community looking for his son, the community realise that they too have been living a lie. Pegeen: 'And to think of the coaxing glory we had given him, and he after doing nothing but hitting a soft blow and chasing northward in a sweat of fear. Quit off from this.'[49] Pegeen and other members of the community had been revitalised and reanimated by Christy's violent story but Synge has employed a cruel, ironic comic reversal. With Pegeen close to tears, Christy makes a farcical attempt to keep things under control: he tries to kill his father in front of the community. Everything that Christy described in his story begins to come to life as he '*runs at OLD MAHON with the loy, chases him out the door, followed by CROWD and WIDOW QUIN. There is a great noise outside, then a yell, and dead silence for a moment.*'[50] The community believe that Old Mahon has been killed as Christy enters the shebeen and sits by the fire, in the exact same way that he did at the beginning of the play: another comic reversal. Now, however, Synge raises the stakes of the drama. He demonstrates that the community's fascination with violence is not based on the fact that they have never been violent themselves, but quite the opposite. They are equally as violent as Christy and they depend on violence to strengthen communal bonds. This is not an idyllic peasant community but a savage pack of individuals. The peasant community proceed to attempt to murder Christy because they are afraid of what the repercussions might be if the police find out that they really have been protecting a murderer: another comic reversal. The community fumble with a rope as they attempt to 'pull a twist on his neck, and squeeze him',[51] while other members of the community – including Pegeen – savagely torture Christy by tying him by the hands and feet and burning his skin with a sod (piece of turf) that has been roasting on the fire. Christy is in agony: '[*kicking and screaming*] Oh, glory be to God!'.[52] Christy is only saved from certain death by the re-re-emergence of his badly wounded father. Old Mahon persuades the community that he will suitably punish his lying son. Such caricature of the Irish peasant and such graphic violence were far too real, even for the leading member of the cast; Willie Fay, who played Christy Mahon, 'begged' Synge to 'take out the torture scene' because it broke 'all the rules of the theatrical game',[53] but Synge would not listen. 'All art is a collaboration',[54] Synge maintained, but that collaboration was now being severely tested. If the Abbey Theatre wanted cottage kitchen realism then Synge would use caricature to define its limits.

Satire

Satire uses humour to ridicule society, often with the hope of ensuring social change. Therefore, for satire to be successful it has to identify social customs and values of society or individual members in a society and hold them up for ridicule. *The Playboy* satirises Irish society's thoughts on class and religion and gender and sexuality, and I will treat these two themes in detail in due course. However, it is important to identify how satire operates in the play from a technical perspective. In order to do this, we must consider Synge's use of indecent jokes.

As stated in the previous chapter, Synge's writing of satire was very much influenced by that of Rabelais and, just like Rabelais's, Synge's satire in *The Playboy* contains indecent jokes and caricature. Many of the indecent jokes in the play are used to provide information about the setting and the characters that are in it. The comic effect of these indecent jokes never becomes clichéd because the language is very descriptive.

Let me give an example. The shebeen in which the play is set is an illegal pub. The owner, Michael James, is looking for a brave security guard. Synge emphasises the shebeen's illegality and Christy's bravery by saying that if Christy were to act as a makeshift security guard then no policeman 'would come smelling around if the dog itself were lapping poteen [illegal alcohol] from the dung-pit of the yard' because they would be afraid of Christy, 'a foxy divil with a pitchpike on the flags of hell'.[55] That is a very elaborate way of emphasising Christy's bravery, and the illegality of the shebeen. In so doing, Synge is satirising the community's cheerful acceptance of illegality. His notebooks reveal that he wrote three moments in *The Playboy* as 'Rabelaisian'.[56] These three moments are: Pegeen and the Widow Quin fighting over Christy in Act I, Widow Quin attempting to remove Old Mahon from the community in Act III and Christy and Pegeen discussing their marriage with Michael James. All three moments contain many indecent jokes that increase satire. Synge thought that the first moment between Pegeen and Widow Quin should be satiri-cally 'very strong',[57] so I will use that moment to explain how satire is built into the structure of the play.

In Act I Widow Quin and Pegeen fight over where, and with whom, Christy should be staying. Each wants Christy to stay with her. The two women begin insulting each other with indecent jokes in order to prove to Christy who is the most ideal candidate for Christy to give his affection to. First of all, the very fact that two women were fighting over a murderer was satirical of the gendered perception that women were conservative and dignified in Synge's Ireland. And then Synge lets the indecent jokes fly. Pegeen accuses the Widow Quin of committing 'a sneaky kind of murder';[58] she 'destroyed her man [her husband]'[59] by hitting him 'with a worn pick, and the rusted poison did corrode his blood'.[60] In response Widow Quin says that Pegeen goes 'helter-skeltering after any man would let [her] a wink upon the road',[61] to which Pegeen replies: 'doesn't the world know you reared a black ram at your own breast, so that the Lord Bishop of Connaught felt the elements of a Christian, and he eating it after in a kidney stew?'.[62] Essentially, Pegeen accuses her neighbour of being a *real* murderer and for using dark magic and sin to trick and fool the Catholic Church, and Widow Quin accuses Pegeen of falling at the feet of any man who happens to wink at her as she passes him on the road. Notice these indecent jokes are very much dependent on caricature. Significantly, neither Pegeen nor Widow Quin denies these jokes, which allows us to think that they have some basis in reality. This is precisely what satire is: indecent jokes that painfully exaggerate and expose social realities.

It is significant that Synge writes his play with a colourful language that was satirical of the perception of how people, let alone women, spoke in the west of Ireland. However, Synge is not satirising for the sake of being funny; it is to deconstruct the power of society to create stereotypes. He uses satire to expose the reality behind the illusion of the stereotype, and in so doing *The Playboy* is dedicated to achieving social change. Synge wants us to think carefully about whether or not the peasantry in the west of Ireland were as virtuous as the conventions of society had made them out to be. The comic devices of reversals, farce and caricature are absolutely integral to understanding how the play satirises its two major subjects: class and religion, and gender and sexuality. Synge uses all of these comic devices to deconstruct social perspectives on these subjects in the Ireland of his time. Ultimately, by deconstructing these subjects Synge is able to foreground the play's major theme: the problematic gap between illusion and reality. He uses comic devices to ask us to confront a timeless question: are dominant social attitudes to class, religion, gender and sexuality an illusion, or a profound reality? And it is to these two key subjects in the play that I will now turn my attention.

Class and religion

The Playboy is a calculated attack on the Catholic middle class in Synge's Ireland. His premier object of classed and religious satire in the play is the character of Shawn Keogh. Shawn is the symbolic representation of the Catholic middle classes in the play: he is a strong farmer. Synge is careful to demonstrate the economic strength of Shawn's farm throughout the play; in the cast list Shawn is listed as a 'farmer', whereas two minor characters in the community – Philly and Jimmy – are characterised as 'small farmers'.[63] Small farmers in Synge's Ireland were newly enfranchised peasant farmers who largely grew potato crops. Throughout the play Shawn uses the surplus capital from his farm to make deals with Michael James for Pegeen's hand in marriage, and with the Widow Quin for her help to remove Christy from the community. So that he can marry Pegeen, Shawn offers Michael James a 'drift of heifers and [his] blue bull from Sneem';[64] he offers the Widow Quin 'a ewe . . . the red cow . . . and the mountainy ram, and the right of way across [his] rye path, and a load of dung at Michaelmas, and turbary [turf] upon the western hill'.[65] In private Synge detested characters like Shawn Keogh as being weak and corrupt individuals. Synge saw Shawn Keogh in what he described as 'the groggy-patriot-publican-general-shop-man who is married to the priest's half-sister and is second cousin once-removed of the dispensary doctor', concluding that these characters are 'swindling the people themselves in a dozen ways . . . it's beastly . . . [they have] a rampant, double-chinned vulgarity I haven't seen the like of'.[66] This is precisely why Synge chooses to dramatise Shawn as a pathetic character, because in so doing he satirises the Catholic middle classes. Synge uses two strategies to demonstrate that Shawn is pathetic: the juxtaposition of Christy's class with Shawn's, and a scathing attack on Roman Catholicism. Significantly, because Shawn is a representative of the Catholic middle classes then *The Playboy* essentially satirised its own audience, the Catholic middle classes being the dominant spectators at the Abbey Theatre.

In the cast list for the play Old Mahon is characterised as 'a squatter',[67] which by implication makes Christy a squatter too. A squatter in Synge's Ireland was a wandering tramp and, indeed, the tramp-like nature of Christy and his father is continually referred to throughout the play. For example, Shawn says that Pegeen is guilty of 'picking a dirty tramp up from the highways of the world',[68] and when the Widow Quin first sees Old Mahon, she refers to him as 'that tramper'.[69] Christy's claim that he is 'the son of a strong farmer'[70] with 'wide and windy acres of rich Munster land'[71] is just part of his elaborate lie. The truth is that he has been 'walking wild for eleven days'[72] to be found 'in the furzy ditch, groaning wicked like a maddening dog', with his 'whole skin needing washing like a Wicklow sheep'.[73] However, the community actually believes that Christy is a strong Catholic farmer and, in many respects, he appears to be a strong-willed version of the weak-willed Shawn. This is why Pegeen refers to Shawn as 'a middling kind of scarecrow with no savagery or fine words in him at all'.[74] Even when Michael James is about to give his blessing to Christy and Pegeen's marriage, he asks 'are you not jealous at all?', to which Shawn replies '[*in great misery*] I'd be afeard to be jealous of a man did slay his da.'[75] By ridiculing Shawn's pathetic nature Synge is satirising the perceived socio-economic superiority of the Catholic middle classes and, in allowing the community to believe that Christy-the-tramp is actually Christy-the-son-of-a-strong-farmer, Synge exposes the rise of the Catholic middle classes as a lie, a complete fiction that has no bearing on reality. Christy-the-tramp is full of ambition, desire and free will because he is a tramp; he does not have to conform to any superficial classed stereotype like Shawn Keogh. It is important to note that at the farcical ending of the play, Synge still privileges the stereotype of Christy-the-tramp as being victorious: 'I'm master of all fights from now.'[76] Synge has used satire and farce to deconstruct the tramp's worthless socio-economic status; the stereotype has been changed. In contrast, Shawn has not changed at all. He lacks ambition, desire and agency because he is afraid of breaking the moral code that defines his socio-economic status: Shawn, who 'would wear the spirits from the saints of peace',[77] lacks Christy's courage because of his strict adherence to Roman Catholicism.

The Playboy satirises Roman Catholicism's influence on class in Synge's Ireland and also Roman Catholicism as an orthodox religion. At the beginning of the play we are told that for the marriage between Pegeen and Shawn to take place, a 'dispensation from the bishops or the Court of Rome' is needed.[78] A dispensation is granted by the Catholic Church in order to excuse and allow members of the Church to do something that breaks canon law, such as intermarriage between cousins; in the cast list for the play Shawn Keogh is characterised as Pegeen's 'second cousin'.[79] If we recall that Synge despised the Catholic middle classes for their inbreeding (the groggy-patriot-publican-general-shop-man who is married to the priest's half-sister and is second cousin once-removed of the dispensary doctor')[80] then, right from the beginning of the play, Synge makes his point very clearly: the Catholic Church is just as corrupt as the Catholic middle classes in Ireland. This is why Shawn reminds Michael James that they have struck 'a good bargain'[81] for Pegeen's hand in marriage, a bargain that is worth the potential communal shame the family face from intermarrying. However, Pegeen laughs at Shawn's appeal to the Catholic Church for a dispensation:

> it's a wonder, Shaneen, the Holy Father'd be taking notice of the likes of you, for if I was him, I wouldn't bother with this place where you'll meet none but Red Linahan, has a squint in his eye, and Patcheen is lame in his heel, or the mad Mulrannies were driven from California and

they lost in their wits. We're a queer lot these times to go troubling the Holy Father on his sacred seat.[82]

This is because Synge dramatises the Mayo community as 'swearing Christians'.[83]

When Shawn threatens the sinful community with 'the curse of the priest' and 'the scarlet-coated bishops of the courts of Rome',[84] they sit back and laugh. Christian morals and ethics have no place here. This is why the previous arrival of 'holy missioners making sermons of the villainy of man'[85] have confused the community. However, a son who murdered his father makes perfect sense. Significantly, Synge demonstrates that it isn't simply this community in Mayo that is devoid of Christian morals and ethics; it is the entire country of Ireland. The community reference how 'holy Luthers of the preaching North' have been known to 'marry three wives'.[86] Father Reilly, the Catholic parish priest, has absolutely no power in the community. Throughout the play, Synge is very careful to ensure that he never appears onstage. Father Reilly's absence is his presence, and we begin to ask ourselves, why doesn't Father Reilly put a stop to the acceptance of a murderer in his parish? Father Reilly is fully aware that Christy is in the community: 'I'm after meeting Shawn Keogh and Father Reilly', says the Widow Quin, and they 'told me of your curiosity man, and they fearing by this time he was maybe roaring, romping on your hands with drink'.[87] It becomes clear that Father Reilly cannot control the community because the Catholic Church is a joke. For example, upon finding Christy's boots in the shebeen, one of the village girls (Sara Tansey) thinks about wearing them 'for walking to the priest, you'd be ashamed this place, going up winter and summer with nothing worth while to confess at all'.[88] However, earlier in the play members of the community cheerfully reference murder and torture as hobbies: 'Marcus Quin, God rest him, got six months for maiming ewes.'[89] According to Catholic doctrine, there is *a lot* to confess in this place. However, Pegeen puts the situation to Shawn Keogh (the only character who actually listens to Father Reilly) very bluntly: 'stop tormenting me with Father Reilly'.[90] All of these minor jokes are used by Synge to foreground the biggest joke of them all: the community's complete nonchalance over Christy's attempted murder of his father.

Christy's admission of patricide is the play's biggest attack on Catholic religion:

CHRISTY. . . . I killed my poor father, Tuesday was a week, for doing the like of that.
PEGEEN. [*with blank amazement*] Is it killed your father?
CHRISTY. [*subsiding*] With the help of God I did surely, and that the Holy Immaculate Mother may intercede for his soul.[91]

Not only did Christy kill his father, but also he believed that God helped him. Furthermore, he asks the Virgin Mary to ensure that his 'deceased' father can enter heaven. At the end of the play, Shawn says, 'it's a miracle Father Reilly can wed us in the end of all'.[92] It certainly is a miracle, on account of how much sin flows through the community. But Synge's satire of the Catholic Church hasn't quite ended. The final line of the play is Pegeen's: '[*putting on her shawl over her head and breaking out into wild lamentations*] Oh my grief, I've lost him surely. I've lost my playboy of the western world.'[93] Here, Pegeen is performing the *caoine* (keen): a lament for the dead with a history that goes back to pre-Christian Ireland. Synge first encountered the *caoine* on the Aran Islands in 1899, and he characterises it as 'the cries of pagan desperation'.[94] The Catholic devotional revolution in Ireland attempted to erase any performance of the *caoine* because, in an age of Darwinism, it was an index for a pre-modern culture that had failed to evolve. It was expected that lamentation and mourning should be performed in a church and, furthermore, within an orthodox Catholic structure – not a pagan anti-structure complete with wild lamentations. Writing from New York, the patron of the Abbey Theatre, John Quinn, stated how 'the attacks of the milk-fed lambs of the convents and Christian Brothers' schools filled me with rage and loathing at the hypocrisy that is so prevalent in Irish life today'.[95] Quinn's thoughts on the hypocrisy of the Catholic Church in Ireland are clearly in line with Synge's. What the Church at this time held in highest regard was a strict set of rules around gender and sexuality. Violence and obscenity, class and religion are very clearly foregrounded as comedy by Synge in the play. But it also completes a daring hat-trick: conservative attitudes to gender and sexuality are also seen as something to be laughed at.

Gender and sexuality

Gender is a fluid concept that helps construct masculinity and femininity. Sexuality is also a fluid concept that helps define sexual preference. *The Playboy* satirised Catholic Ireland's conservative attitudes towards both of these concepts. In the Ireland of Synge's time, women held a conservative gendered position within a patriarchal society: they were expected to be seen and not heard, and they were certainly not to be associated with sex. Synge first got into trouble when criticising Ireland's conservative attitudes to gender and sexuality in 1903, when his play *In the Shadow of the Glen* was first performed. In that play an unfaithful wife is banished from her home by her husband, and she leaves with a tramp. There was absolute mayhem when Synge first staged that play. Arthur Griffith and Sinn Féin led the attacks, maintaining that Irish women were not capable of doing such a thing: 'all of us know – that Irishwomen are the most virtuous women in the world'.[96] *The Playboy* proceeded to demonstrate that Irish women were not that virtuous at all. Old Mahon summarises the situation well: 'is it in a crazy-house for females that I'm landed now?'.[97]

Catholic Ireland expected women to behave in accordance with a strict patriarchal code: they should be good wives, loving mothers, and above all wholly innocent. This is why Shawn says of Christy: 'that'd be a queer kind to bring into a decent household with the like of Pegeen Mike'.[98] Unmarried women could never be left alone with a man, least of all overnight. Synge uses comic caricature to ridicule female gender and sexuality through the characters of Pegeen and Widow Quin. He is careful to write Pegeen's character as the opposite of the gendered perception of women by inverting her gender and playing with her sexuality. Pegeen is fiercely independent 'with the divil's own temper',[99] and she has complete power over men in the play. Furthermore, Pegeen is said to be always 'itching and scratching, and she with a stale stink of poteen on her selling in the shop'.[100] Synge deliberately leaves the reason as to Pegeen's continual itching and scratching open to doubt. It could be because she has poor personal hygiene, or even worse that she has a sexually transmitted disease; after all, Pegeen has been known to 'go helter-skeltering after any man would let [her] a wink upon the road'.[101] Both conclusions as to why Pegeen is itching and scratching were tabooed in Synge's Ireland; it was bad enough that a woman would smell of stale alcohol.

Widow Quin talks openly about her attraction to the 'gallant hairy fellows drifting beyond'[102] – that is, the heroic, hairy men who are in the community. As I have already demonstrated, the Widow has killed the patriarch in her life: she 'destroyed her man'[103] by hitting him 'with a worn pick, and the rusted poison did corrode his blood'.[104] Synge's point is clear: women in this community are sexually devious, and unlike the men, they don't pretend to be something they are not. In Synge's Ireland, male gender and sexuality is an illusion. Old Mahon reveals the reality about his son's gender and sexuality: if Christy saw a woman

> he'd be off to hide in the sticks, and you'd see him shooting out his sheep's eyes between the little twigs and leaves, and his two ears rising like a hare looking out through a gap. Girls indeed! . . . wasn't he the laughing joke of every female woman.[105]

The Playboy is a play about strong matriarchs, or women behaving like patriarchs in a society where the traditional understanding of masculinity is an absolute joke. This is why, even at the end of the play, when Shawn talks about how his marriage to Pegeen looks as though it is going to happen after all, Pegeen immediately responds: '[*hitting him a box on the ear*] Quit my sight.'[106]

Synge also uses caricature to satirise what he perceives to be the inbreeding among the Catholic middle classes. Christy tells us the reason why he hit his father:

We were digging spuds in his cold, sloping, stony divil's patch of a field . . . there I was, digging and digging, and 'You squinting idiot', says he, 'let you walk down now and tell the priest you'll wed the Widow Casey in a score of days . . . [She was] a walking terror from beyond the hills, and she two score and five years, and two hundred-weights and five pounds in the weighing skills, with a limping leg on her, and a blinded eye, and she a woman of noted misbehaviour with the old and young . . . . 'I won't wed her', says I, 'when all know she did suckle me for six weeks when I came into the world, and she a hag this day with a tongue on her has the crows and seabirds scattered, the way they wouldn't cast a shadow on her garden with the dread of her curse.'[107]

If we recall that Christy pretends to be from a middle-class Catholic family, then Synge deliberately makes the point that men from the Catholic middle classes are known for marrying the same women who breast-fed them. Notice also how Synge caricatures women as being virtuous: the Widow Casey is not described as being either physically or mentally attractive. She is also known for being sexually promiscuous with all ages.

The premier offence against gender and sexuality in the play is Christy's farcical attempt to keep Pegeen from withdrawing her affections for him: 'it's Pegeen I'm seeking only, and what'd I care if you brought me a drift of chosen females, standing in their shifts itself maybe, from this place to the Eastern World'.[108] On the opening night of the play, Lady Gregory wrote a telegram to W. B. Yeats putting the situation bluntly: 'audience broke up in disorder at the word shift'.[109] The word 'shift' in Synge's Ireland was as an extremely colloquial phrase for a lady's underwear. On seeing the play, a 'western girl' wrote into the national newspaper complaining of Synge's use of the word:

> Dublin, January 27. '07.
>
> Dear Sir
>
> As an Irishwoman, I desire to enter a most emphatic pro-test against Mr. J. M. Synge's new comedy, 'The Playboy of the Western World'.
>
> . . . We have now an Irish dramatist putting on the boards of Dublin theatre a play representing Irish peo-ple actively sympathising with a parricide, while Irish girls fling themselves into his arms, and an Irish peasant woman, who has made herself a widow, proving her-self to be a liar, an intriguer, and a coarse-spoken virago whose honesty is purchasable at the price of a red cow . . . Miss Allgood (one of the most charming actresses I have ever seen) is forced, before the most fashionable audience in Dublin, to use a word indicating an essential item of female attire, which the lady would probably never utter in ordinary circumstances, even to herself.
>
> [. . .]
>
> – Yours truly,
>
> A Western Girl.[110]

What made matters worse was that Christy's declaration of his love to Pegeen was comparable to not one woman stand-ing in her underwear, but a 'drift' of women. The word 'drift' was also a colloquial phrase for a herd of cattle, and earlier in the play Shawn Keogh used it to refer explicitly to his own cattle.[111] An argument could be made for Synge's decision to employ the word 'shift' so that it could rhyme with the word 'drift' in the same sentence, thereby increasing the musicality of his Hiberno-English dialect. Even still, the word 'shift' and its association with a herd of semi-naked women was particularly offensive. Synge reminded his critics that Douglas Hyde, a founding member of the Gaelic League, had used the word 'shift' – albeit in Irish – in his work *The Love Songs of Connacht*. The critics did not buy Synge's defence. He knew that it had the potential to shock his audience. In private, Synge wrote to his good friend Stephen MacKenna about his thoughts on gender and sexuality in his plays: 'I restored the sex-element to its natural place, and the people were so surprised they saw the sex only . . . I think squeamishness is a disease and that Ireland will gain if Irish writers deal manfully, directly, and decently with the entire reality of life.'[112] Again, we come back to the problems of staging reality within realism. Certainly, Synge's satire of gender and sexuality in *The Playboy* was completely against the dominant ideology in conservative, Catholic Ireland.

Synge believed that 'where a country loses its humour, as some towns in Ireland are doing, there will be morbidity of mind'.[113] As the next chapter demonstrates, when the play went into performance, a lot of Synge's jokes fell flat. But as Synge wrote to the editor of the *Irish Times*, you were either laughing with him or at him in *The Playboy*: 'that is often the case, I think, with comedy'.[114]

Notes

1   *CW*, Vol. IV, 169.
2   NLI MS, 1805, Vol. I, 26 January 1907, fo. 65.

3 Leo Benedictus, 'What to Say about . . . *The Playboy of the Western World*', *Guardian*, 3 October 2011, http://www. theguardian. com/culture/2011/oct/03/playboy-of-the-western-world (accessed 20 November 2015).
4 *CW*, Vol. IV, 87.
5 Ibid., 69.
6 Ibid., 53.
7 Ibid., 53–54.
8 TCD MS 4402, fo. 1r–v.
9 *CW*, Vol. IV, 75.
10 TCD MS 4407, fo. 4v.
11 *CW*, Vol. IV, 141.
12 TCD MS 4392, fo. 10v.
13 *CW*, Vol. IV, 109.
14 TCD MS 4391, fo. 8r.
15 *CW*, Vol. IV, 83.
16 TCD MS 4392, fo. 12v.
17 Ibid., fo. 12r.
18 *CW*, Vol. IV, 73.
19 Ibid., 59.
20 Ibid., 53.
21 *CW*, Vol. II, 224n.
22 Ibid.
23 *CW*, Vol. IV, 73.
24 *CW*, Vol. II, 224n.
25 *CW*, Vol. IV, 67.
26 Ibid., 73.
27 Ibid.
28 Ibid.
29 Ibid.
30 Ibid., 103.
31 Ibid.
32 TCD MS 4405, fo. 10v.
33 TCD MS 4395, fo. 1r.
34 *CW*, Vol. IV, 296.
35 Ibid., 65.
36 Ibid.
37 Ibid., 131.

38 Ibid., 167.
39 Ibid.
40 TCD MS 4405, fo. 10v.
41 *CW*, Vol. IV, 53.
42 Ibid., 54.
43 Ibid., 3.
44 Ibid., 137.
45 Ibid., 59.
46 Ibid., 61.
47 Ibid., 56. See TCD MS 4395, fo. 42v.
48 'The Abbey Theatre', *Freeman's Journal*, 28 January 1907.
49 *CW*, Vol. IV, 161.
50 Ibid., 165.
51 Ibid., 169.
52 Ibid., 171.
53 W. G. Fay and Catherine Carswell, *The Fays of the Abbey Theatre: An Autobiographical Record* (London: Rich and Cowan, 1935), 212.
54 *CW*, Vol. IV, 54.
55 Ibid., 75.
56 Ibid., 296–297.
57 Ibid., 296.
58 Ibid., 89.
59 Ibid., 131.
60 Ibid., 89.
61 Ibid.
62 Ibid.
63 Ibid., 55.
64 Ibid., 155.
65 Ibid., 117.
66 *CW*, Vol. II, 283n.
67 *CW*, Vol. IV, 55.
68 Ibid., 155.
69 Ibid., 119.
70 Ibid., 69.
71 Ibid., 79.
72 Ibid.
73 Ibid., 77.

 74 Ibid., 153.
 75 Ibid., 153, 155.
 76 Ibid., 173.
 77 Ibid., 127
 78 *CW*, Vol. II, 59.
 79 Ibid., 55.
 80 Ibid., 283n.
 81 *CW*, Vol. IV, 59.
 82 Ibid.
 83 Ibid., 94.
 84 Ibid., 65.
 85 Ibid., 71.
 86 Ibid.
 87 Ibid., 87.
 88 Ibid., 97.
 89 Ibid., 59.
 90 Ibid.
 91 Ibid., 73.
 92 Ibid., 173.
 93 Ibid.
 94 *CW*, Vol. II, 75.
 95 John Quinn to F. J. Gregg, 1 April 1909, NYPL, Foster–Murphy
     Collection, MS 251.
 96 Arthur Griffith, untitled response to W. B. Yeats, 'The Irish
     National Theatre and Three Sorts of Ignorance', *United
     Irishman*, 24 October 1903.
 97 *CW*, Vol. IV, 143.
 98 Ibid., 75.
 99 Ibid., 115.
100 Ibid., 127.
101 Ibid., 89.
102 Ibid., 127.
103 Ibid., 131.
104 Ibid., 89.
105 Ibid., 123.
106 Ibid., 173.
107 Ibid., 101, 103.
108 Ibid., 167.

109 Gregory, *Our Irish Theatre*, 112.
110 'A Western Girl', 'To the Editor of the *Freeman's Journal*', *Freeman's Journal*, 28 January 1907.
111 *CW*, Vol. IV, 155.
112 J. M. Synge to Stephen MacKenna, 28 January 1904, *CL*, Vol. I, 74.
113 *CW*, Vol. IV, 3.
114 J. M. Synge to the editor of the *Irish Times*, 30 January 1907, *CL*, Vol. I, 286.

3

Performance

This chapter analyses the first performances of the play before exploring its performance history in the twentieth and twenty-first centuries. A common mistake is to consider the reception of the first performances in January 1907 as a riot. This chapter will demonstrate that while the reception of *The Playboy* was hostile, it was far from a riot.

1907

'As I cast eyes over the script of *The Playboy of the Western World* I knew we were in for serious trouble', wrote Willie Fay, who played Christy Mahon.[1] Rehearsals began on 2 January with the first two acts of the play. Synge provided the third and final act in the following week. The Abbey kept a strict control on who could attend rehearsals, but one person who did manage to make it into the rehearsal room was Oliver St John Gogarty, a doctor and poet. He recalled how Synge 'sat silent, holding his stick between his knees, his chin resting on his hands', and when he asked Synge if the play was just 'a satire to show up, for one thing, how lifeless and inert was the country', Synge snapped:

> he gave me a short glance and looked straight in front of himself, weighing me up and thinking how hard it would be to get the public to appreciate his play as a work of art, when one who should know better was reading analogies and satire into it already. He shook my question off with a shake of his head.[2]

Tensions were running high.

Synge's fellow directors at the Abbey, Lady Gregory and W. B. Yeats, pleaded with him to remove some of the blasphemous language in the play. Synge agreed to remove Pegeen's insult of Widow Quin: 'doesn't the world know you reared a black ram at your own breast, so that the Lord Bishop of Connaught felt the elements of a Christian, and he eating it after in a kidney stew?';[3] but before opening night Synge inserted the line back into the play: in the face of censorship, art was standing tall. Gregory perfectly stated Synge's attitude: 'a tiger with its cub'.[4] At the end of rehearsals Synge wrote to Gregory that 'everything has gone smoothly'.[5]

In 1906 the Abbey dropped the ticket prices to the pit (the seating area directly in front of the stage): they were previously 1s; now they were 6d. What this meant was that people who were used to going to melodrama and pantomime (by far the dominant form of theatre in Synge's Dublin) could now afford to go the Abbey. In melodrama and pantomime actors were used to spectators shouting at the stage. However, the Abbey Theatre staged theatre for the sake of art, and the actors were not prepared for the behaviour of this new audience. Furthermore, by dropping the prices to the seats in the pit, the Abbey Theatre effectively opened their doors to all those members of Sinn Féin and the Gaelic League who could not afford to go to the theatre, but had heard that Synge's three previous plays were damaging to cultural nationalism. On the morning of the first performance Synge wrote to Gregory: 'I most feverently hope it will go off well and be a credit to both of us.'[6] Synge would need much more than hope. All 562 seats in the theatre had been sold. Gregory's response to Synge was entirely appropriate: 'we are beginning the fight for our lives'.[7]

The first performance began at fifteen minutes past eight. The first act was received with applause. The second was received with confusion because of the crude language, but Gregory sent a telegram to Yeats, who was lecturing in Aberdeen, Scotland: 'play great success'.[8] In the third act there was some booing and shouting at the stage when Christy attempted to kill Old Mahon for the second time. Nevertheless, the performance was just minutes from being over. And then, Willie Fay made a very bad mistake with his line 'what'd I care if you brought me a drift of chosen females, standing in their shifts'.[9] As Joseph Holloway recalled in his diary, 'Mayo girls' was substituted for 'chosen females'.[10] The direct reference to women in County Mayo standing in their underwear was an appalling attack on Irish society's conservative attitude to gender and sexuality. Gregory sent another telegram to Yeats: 'audience broke up in disorder at the word "shift"'.[11] Although the performance ended quite quickly after this, Synge's indecent jokes were enough for word to spread throughout Dublin. Holloway summarised popular opinion in his diary:

I maintain that this play of <u>The Playboy</u> is not a truthful or just picture of the Irish peasants, but simply the outpouring of a morbid, unhealthy mind ever seeking on the dungheap of life for the nastiness that lies concealed there.[12]

The theatre was closed on Sunday. However, during the performances on Monday and Tuesday total chaos reigned.

On Monday evening disturbances were organised by the Gaelic League and Sinn Féin. However, approximately 80 seats out of a possible 562 were sold. We should never forget that the debate over *The Playboy* bypassed a large amount of Dublin, let alone Irish life. The second the performance began the spectators began stomping their feet so much that Willie Fay completely broke character and told the spectators that he was originally from County Mayo, and that if order was not resumed then the police would be called for. The shouting at the stage only increased. It was not possible to hear more than six consecutive lines of the play. Synge and George Roberts (an actor in the Society) attempted to silence those spectators who were now cursing at the stage. Roberts recalled: 'in the middle of the commotion I noticed a gleam of humour come into [Synge's] eye, as he took a mental note of a specially violent curse'.[13] If Synge's spectators were offended by his indecent language, then art was mirroring life. However, by now, the performance happening among the spectators was far more interesting than what was happening onstage.

During the performance a young doctor, Daniel Sheehan, approached Synge, saying that he could 'hardly keep himself from jumping on to a seat, and pointing out in that howling mob those whom he [was] treating for venereal disease'.[14]

However, when Christy was tortured with fire, Sheehan decided to offer a different performance analysis: 'what about Tipperary where the witch was burned?'.[15] In 1895, in South Tipperary, Bridget Cleary was tortured and burned alive by her husband because she was believed to be a fairy, and while Bridget was tortured she was accused of being a witch. Bridget Cleary's horrific death damaged middle-class nationalists' bid for political independence from Britain: why should independence be given to a country that tortured those accused of witchcraft and burned supposed fairies alive? Consequently, the 'Tipperary witch-burning' was a social taboo. In performance *The Playboy* succeeded in doing everything that satire should do: the release of social anxiety, and the inversion of social norms in the pursuit of change. The police were eventually called for on Monday night, but when they arrived they were sent away because there was nothing to indicate clearly that a riot was taking place.

Tuesday night's performance was the closest that the reception of the play could come to being considered a riot. On Tuesday morning Yeats fuelled the flames of discontent by telling one newspaper that those who rioted had 'no books in their houses'.[16] Privately, Lady Gregory admitted that the Abbey was in a battle 'between those who use a toothbrush and those who don't'.[17] As a precautionary measure the police lined the aisles of the pit of the theatre on Tuesday night. At the beginning of the performance a man from County Galway addressed the entire theatre, and particularly those who were preparing to disturb the performance, challenging them to a fight: 'Come on, any of you', said the man, to which the disturbers replied, 'we could wipe the streets with you'.[18] The man responded: 'I am a little bit drunk and don't know what I am saying', before playing a random mix of off-key notes on the piano in the orchestra. Synge eventually asked the man to leave, which he did. As he was leaving, students from Trinity College Dublin – a quintessential Anglo-Irish Ascendancy institution – arrived to support the play written by an Anglo-Irish Ascendancy playwright. One of the students was Lady Gregory's nephew; she had asked him to come to the performance and bring 'a few fellow athletes' in case of 'an attack on the stage'.[19] The students were seated in the gallery, and they taunted members of Sinn Féin and the Gaelic League below them in the pit by singing the English national anthem. Those taunted responded with 'The West's Asleep', a famous Irish rebel song. The battle for cultural expression was now being fought between Catholic Ireland and Ascendancy Ireland.

When the performance eventually started the audience began stomping their feet and shouting at the stage from the moment Christy entered. The police immediately attempted to make arrests as the orchestra played jaunty, vaudeville tunes, and Yeats took to the stage and lectured the spectators on the importance of art. This was not a riot but an elaborate farce. As the police ran through the aisles to audience laughter, the man from Galway arrived back in the theatre, completely drunk, and began making his presence known. As one newspaper put it, 'from start to finish not half a dozen consecutive sentences had been heard by the audience'.[20] All of this frustration and aggression spilled out of the theatre and onto Dublin's city-centre streets, where a small fight took place on Westmoreland Street, but only one arrest was made. *The Playboy* had become a national scandal.

By Wednesday morning the disturbers were being fined in court, a judicial process that would take place again on Friday. On Wednesday night approximately 420 seats were sold. There was more shouting at the stage. However, when the character of Philly in the play said 'I'm thinking we'll have right sport, before night will fall',[21] the entire theatre 'joined in an outburst of hearty laughter'[22] because the spectators were there to perform for each other rather than to watch the play. A singular fight broke out front of house between an Englishman and an Irishman, further exacerbating the point that the play was written by an Ascendancy playwright. However, the spectators made their way out into the Dublin night air without any further altercation. The performances for the rest of the week were relatively tame in comparison, so much so that the *Irish Times* commented how 'there was a remarkable change in the attitude of the audience at the Abbey Theatre' for Thursday night's performance.[23] *The Playboy*'s final performance on Saturday 2 February was uninterrupted.

On the Monday following the final performance the Abbey Theatre decided to hold a debate entitled 'The Freedom of the Theatre', in which people could debate the importance of artistic expression. Synge decided against going because he thought it was pointless trying to reason with 'low ruffians' who were not 'men of intellect and honesty'.[24] Yeats began the debate, discussing the value of art, but his passionate plea was falling on deaf ears; one debater stood up and firmly objected to Yeats's 'theory of dragooning people into one's theories of art'.[25] However, one person who attended the debate was Daniel Sheehan, who 'claimed his right to speak as a medical student'.[26] Sheehan offered his full support of the play: 'Mr Synge had drawn a type of character that ever since he had studied any science he had paid strong attention to, and that was the sexual melancholia', and 'in any country town in Ireland [one] would get types of men like Christy Mahon'.[27] Sheehan continued: 'when the artist appears in Ireland who was not afraid of life and his nature, the women of Ireland would receive him'. As Sheehan said this the reporter for the *Freeman's Journal* watched as 'many ladies whose countenances plainly indicated intense feelings of astonishment and pain, rose and left the place. Many men also retired.'[28]

Just like the play, the reception to the performance contained comic reversals, caricatures and farcical moments. This was the greatest review that *The Playboy* could have received; the violence and obscenity that Synge wrote about in his illusory world came to life. Remember, the play asks us to think about the problem of when illusions become reality. It is therefore very significant that it had a profound impact on reality through the greatest illusion of all: performance. What the play demonstrated in performance was something that Christy Mahon had figured out a long time ago: the truth is best said as a fiction.

After 1907

On 11 May 1907, the Abbey Theatre toured *The Playboy* to the United Kingdom, arriving in London on 9 June. The play was 'carefully pruned of too frequently reoccurring expletives, and, as revised, met with a favourable reception'.[29] However, in 1911 when *The Playboy* toured to North America the disturbances resumed. The *Gaelic American* asked for the help of 'every decent Irish man and woman, and of the Catholic Church, whose doctrines and devotional practices are held up to scorn and ridicule in Synge's monstrosity'.[30] The problem with *The Playboy* in North America was the same as that in Ireland: the politics of identity. Irish emigrants to North America didn't want their new-found identity to be defined by the stereotypes in Synge's play. When the play opened in

Paris at the Théâtre de L'Oeuvre in 1913, it caused a scandal because of its satirisation of the Catholic Church.

As the twentieth century progressed into an age of extremes, Synge's satire on the Ireland of his time naturally lost some of its cutting edge. Nevertheless, in performance the play had an uncanny resemblance to life offstage. For example, in 1975 spectators at the Royal National Theatre in London watched Synge's representation of violent people in Ireland as the IRA violently pursued their campaign to restore the six counties of Northern Ireland to the Irish Republic. On the opening night of the performance a restaurant in London's Mayfair district was bombed by the IRA. Once again, the illusion of performance was frighteningly real.

Druid Theatre Company from Galway in Ireland are often thought to be a company that produce a 'faithful' representation of the play. *The Playboy* was the first play they performed when the company formed in 1975. In 1982 they performed it again, taking the performance to the Aran Islands before embarking on a three-year international tour. Tackling sexuality and violence with graphic realism, the performance was instrumental in reminding the world of Synge's talent as a playwright. Other performances of note by the company include their 2004 performance with Hollywood actor Cillian Murphy as Christy Mahon. The play was revived in 2005 (without Cillian Murphy) as part of the company's ambitious project to stage six of Synge's seven plays in a one-day cycle known as DruidSynge. The *Irish Times* remarked that Druid 'gave us an all-but definitive version of *Playboy*'.[31]

The play has also received topical adaptations to deal with the politics of identity in other countries. The first of these was Mustapha Matura's *Playboy of the West Indies*, which opened at the Oxford Playhouse in 1984. In 2006 a company from

Dublin, Pan Pan Theatre, wanted to see how well *The Playboy* could translate to the eastern world. Directed by Gavin Quinn, the play premiered in Beijing with an all-Chinese cast performing in Mandarin. In this version of Synge's play a Muslim farm worker from Xinjiang Province arrived at a Beijing 'whoredresser's', a brothel that posed as a hairdresser's. The *Irish Times* pointed out that

> the similarities between China now and Ireland then are striking. Ireland in the time of Synge's play was changing rapidly – urbanization was beginning in earnest, the country grappling with modernity. The scale may be hugely different, but similar forces are at work in China.[32]

Quinn used stylised movement from Chinese opera to compliment Synge's stylised language. Spectators complained to the Chinese Ministry of Culture, believing that the production was far too sexual, and just like in January 1907, the police were sent to the theatre. However, the police did not press charges. When the performance came to Dublin later that year, English surtitles were used. *The Playboy* in Chinese was familiar and yet very unfamiliar to spectators in Dublin. Now Synge's play was being used to question the reality and illusion of the effects of globalisation and interculturalism. These themes were further explored in an adaptation of the play by Bisi Adigun and Roddy Doyle at the Abbey Theatre in 2007. In this production Christy Mahon was adapted to Christopher Malomo, a Yoruba man from western Nigeria. Malomo 'killed' his father with a pestle before arriving in gangland west Dublin seeking asylum. The performance may have turned realism into pantomime, but it brought a sharp focus onto Irish attitudes to interculturalism.

What the production history of *The Playboy* demonstrates is that the play is continually relevant, in whatever context: not simply because the play asks spectators to remove illusions and confront public and private realities, but also because in performance it reminds us of the importance of the power of art in shining a light on uncomfortable truths, often in the darkest of times.

Notes

1   Fay and Carswell, *The Fays of the Abbey Theatre*, 211–212.
2   Oliver St John Gogarty, *As I Was Going down Sackville Street: A Phantasy in Fact* (London: Rich and Cowan, 1937), 282.
3   *CW*, Vol. IV, 89.
4   Lady Augusta Gregory to W. B. Yeats, 12 January 1907, in Yeats, Gregory and J. M. Synge, *Theatre Business: The Correspondence of the First Abbey Theatre Directors: William Butler Yeats, Lady Gregory and J. M. Synge*, ed. Ann Saddlemyer (Gerrards Cross: Colin Smythe, 1982), 205n.
5   J. M. Synge to Lady Augusta Gregory, 26 January 1907, *CL*, Vol. I, 284.
6   Ibid.
7   Lady Augusta Gregory to J. M. Synge, 13 January 1907, in Yeats, Gregory and Synge, *Theatre Business*, 205.
8   Gregory, *Our Irish Theatre*, 112.
9   *CW*, Vol. IV, 167.
10 NLI MS 1805, Vol. I, January 26 1907, fo. 63.
11 Gregory, *Our Irish Theatre*, 112.
12 NLI MS 1805, Vol. I, January 26 1907, fo. 63.
13 George Roberts, 'Memoirs of George Roberts', *Irish Times*, 14 September 1955.
14 W. B. Yeats, *Essays and Introductions* (London: Macmillan, 1961), 312.
15 'Police In'.
16 'Abbey Theatre Scene', *Evening Telegraph*, 29 January 1907.

17 Lady Augusta Gregory, quoted in Colm Tóibín, *Lady Gregory's Toothbrush* (London: Picador, 2002), 65.
18 'Abbey Theatre Scenes', *Freeman's Journal*, 30 January 1907.
19 Gregory, *Our Irish Theatre*, 114.
20 'Abbey Theatre Scenes'.
21 *CW*, Vol. IV, 145.
22 'The Abbey Theatre', *Freeman's Journal*, 31 January 1907.
23 '*The Playboy of the Western World*', *Irish Times*, 1 February 1907.
24 J. M. Synge to Molly Allgood, 5 February 1907, *CL*, Vol. I, 289.
25 'The Freedom of the Play', *Irish Times*, 5 February 1907.
26 'Parricide and Public Discussion at the Abbey Theatre', *Freeman's Journal*, 5 February 1907.
27 'The Freedom of the Play'.
28 'Parricide and Public Discussion'.
29 'Abbey Theatre', *Irish Times*, 28 May 1909.
30 'Irishmen Will Stamp Out the Playboy', *Gaelic American*, 14 October 1911.
31 Crawley, 'A Decade Framed by Playboys', *Irish Times*, 2 December 2009.
32 Clifford Coonan, 'Playboy of the Eastern World', *Irish Times*, 21 March 2006.

Conclusion

In the immediate days after *The Playboy* finished its run, Synge tried to make sense of everything that happened: 'we're all wild geese, at the bottom, all we players, artists, and writers', Synge wrote to Molly Allgood, 'and there is no keeping us in a back yard like a barndoor fowl. The one point is that when we fly it should be to the North Sea or the Islands of the Blessed, not to some sooty ornamental water in some filthy town.'[1] Synge passionately believed that all artists should be given the freedom to spread their wings. *The Playboy*, however, never got off the ground in Synge's lifetime. In one of his angrier moments he drafted an open letter to the Gaelic League in which he attacked the League for being 'founded on a doctrine that is made up of ignorance, fraud and hypocrisy'.[2] Synge never published the letter because, as he said to his nephew, *The Playboy* would stand the test of time.

Two years after *The Playboy*'s premiere, Synge lay dying in a nursing home in Dublin. On the morning of his death John Butler Yeats simply wrote in his diary that 'John Synge is dead in Dublin' before proceeding to recall the *Playboy* disturbances:

in holes and corners and in whispered colloquies these
disturbers would admit that Synge's picture was a true
rendering; that the facts were true but should not be
revealed to the world. Again, under the curse of subjec-
tion we feared the truth.[3]

W. B. Yeats wrote:

> Synge was the rushing up of the buried fire, an explosion
> of all that had been denied or refused, a furious impar-
> tiality, an indifferent turbulent sorrow. Like Burns, his
> work was to say all the people did not want to have said.[4]

Within the fullness of time, some Irish nationalists such as
Pádraig Pearse came to understand the value of art in *The
Playboy*. Pearse wrote:

> when a man like Synge, a man in whose sad heart glowed
> a true love of Ireland, one of the two or three men who
> have in our time made Ireland considerable in the eyes of
> the world, uses strange symbols which we do not under-
> stand, we cry out that he has blasphemed and we proceed
> to crucify him.[5]

If viewed in the context of Synge's six other plays, *The
Playboy* is part of his wider thoughts on how Ireland should
embrace modernity. Synge believed that if Ireland were to
become a modern nation then it needed to take a long, hard
look in the mirror and address all of the false illusions that
obscured everyday realities. Many other modern Irish playwrights would go on to address this question, but Synge

was the first. For example, in 1926, Seán O'Casey offered the Abbey Theatre an unsympathetic depiction of the reality behind the 1916 Easter Rising in *The Plough and the Stars*. The spectators caused significant disturbances at those performances, too.

Looking over the world playwrights that Synge influenced, from Artaud to Brecht, from Beckett to Carr, what all of these playwrights have in common is their use of theatre to shock spectators into removing public and private illusions and addressing public and private realities. The night after the first performance of *The Playboy* Synge wrote to Molly: 'it is better any day to have the row we had last night, than to have your play fizzling out in half-hearted applause. We're an event in the history of the Irish stage.'[6] *The Playboy* was not simply an event in the history of the Irish stage. It was an event in the history of the world stage.

Notes

1 J. M. Synge to Molly Algood, 22 February 1907, *CL*, Vol. I, 300–301.
2 *CW*, Vol. II, 399.
3 John Butler Yeats, 'John Synge is Dead', NYPL, Foster–Murphy Collection.
4 W. B. Yeats, *The Death of Synge and Other Passages from an Old Diary* (Dublin: Cuala, 1971), 27.
5 P. H. P[earse], 'From a Hermitage', *Irish Freedom*, June 1913.
6 J. M. Synge to Molly Algood, 27 January 1907, *CL*, Vol. I, 285.

Bibliography

Manuscripts

National Library of Ireland

Diaries of Joseph Holloway, Recording Theatrical Performances in Dublin and His Views Thereon, Including Newscuttings and Programmes Relating Thereto, 1900–1909. From 1908, 2 vols. per year. Impressions of a Dublin Playgoer. Vol. I, *January–June 1907.* MS 1805.

'Twenty two letters of John Millington Synge to Max Meyerfeld, translator of Synge's works into German, with one of A. J. Stephens to the same, 1905–1909.' MS 778.

New York Public Library

Foster–Murphy Collection. MS 251.

John Butler Yeats, 'John Synge is Dead'. Foster–Murphy Collection.

Trinity College Dublin

Manuscripts of the Irish Literary Renaissance:
J. M. Synge Manuscripts

Commonplace book, 1894–1895. MS 4379.

Commonplace book, *c.* 1900. MS 4392.

Commonplace book, 1903. MS 4391.
Commonplace book, 1904. MS 4395.
'In West Kerry, September 1905.' MS 4402.
Literary commonplace book, *c.* 1905. MS 4407.
Literary commonplace book, *c.* 1907. MS 4405.

Stephens–Synge Manuscripts

John Synge: Manuscript of the Biography of John Millington Synge by Edward M. Stephens. Fair Copy in Manuscript, Occasional Typed Texts Inserted Especially 1906 Onwards. MS 6191.

Printed works

'The Abbey Theatre', *Freeman's Journal.* 28 January 1907.
'The Abbey Theatre', *Freeman's Journal.* 31 January 1907.
'Abbey Theatre', *Irish Times.* 28 May 1909.
'Abbey Theatre Scene', *Evening Telegraph.* 29 January 1907.
'Abbey Theatre Scenes', *Freeman's Journal.* 30 January 1907.
A. F., 'I Don't Care a Rap', *Dublin Evening Mail.* 29 January 1907.
'Awful Murder of a Father by His Own Son', *Galway Express.* 1 February 1873.
Benedictus, Leo. 'What to Say about . . . *The Playboy of the Western World*', *Guardian.* 3 October 2011.
Carney, James. *The Playboy and The Yellow Lady.* Dublin: Poolbeg, 1986.
Coonan, Clifford. 'Playboy of the Eastern World', *Irish Times*, 21 March 2006.
Crawley, Peter. 'A Decade Framed by Playboys', *Irish Times*, 2 December 2009.
Duncan, Ellen. '*The Playboy.' Irish Times.* 29 January 1907.
Fay, W. G. and Catherine Carswell. *The Fays of the Abbey Theatre: An Autobiographical Record.* London: Rich and Cowan, 1935.
'The Freedom of the Play', *Irish Times.* 5 February 1907.
Gogarty, Oliver St John. *As I Was Going down Sackville Street: A Phantasy in Fact.* London: Rich and Cowan, 1937.
Gregory, Lady Augusta. *Our Irish Theatre.* New York: Capricorn, 1965.

Griffith, Arthur. 'All Ireland', *United Irishman*. 17 October 1903.

Griffith, Arthur, untitled response to W. B. Yeats, 'The Irish National Theatre and Three Sorts of Ignorance.' *United Irishman*, 24 October 1903.

'Irishmen Will Stamp Out the Playboy', *Gaelic American*. 14 October 1911.

Larkin, Emmet. *The Making of the Roman Catholic Church in Ireland: 1850–1860*. Chapel Hill, NC: University of North California Press, 1980.

MacKenna, Stephen. 'Synge', *Irish Statesman*. 3 November 1928.

'Parricide and Public Discussion at the Abbey Theatre', *Freeman's Journal*. 5 February 1907.

Pearse, P. H. 'The Passing of Anglo-Irish Drama', *An Claidheamh Soluis*. 9 February 1907.

P[earse], P. H. 'From a Hermitage', *Irish Freedom*. June 1913.

'*The Playboy of the Western World*', *Irish Times*. 1 February 1907.

'Police In', *Irish Independent*. 29 January 1907.

Roberts, George. 'Memoirs of George Roberts'. *Irish Times*, 14 September 1955.

Synge, J. M. *The Collected Letters of John Millington Synge*. Vol. I, *1871–1907*. Ed. Ann Saddlemyer. Oxford: Clarendon Press, 1983.

Synge, J. M. *Collected Works*. Vol. II, *Prose*. Ed. Alan Price. London: Oxford University Press, 1966.

Synge, J. M. *Collected Works*. Vol. IV, *Plays*, Book II. Ed. Ann Saddlemyer. Gerrards Cross: Colin Smythe, 1982.

'A Terrible Outrage on Achill Island', *Irish Times*. 6 October 1894.

Tóibín, Colm. *Lady Gregory's Toothbrush*. London: Picador, 2002.

'A Western Girl'. 'To the Editor of the *Freeman's Journal*', *Freeman's Journal*. 28 January 1907.

Yeats, W. B. *Autobiographies*. London: Macmillan, 1955.

Yeats, W. B. *The Death of Synge and Other Passages from an Old Diary*. Dublin: Cuala, 1971.

Yeats, W. B. *Essays and Introductions*. London: Macmillan, 1961.

Yeats, W. B, Lady Augusta Gregory and J. M. Synge. *Theatre Business: The Correspondence of the First Abbey Theatre Directors: William Butler Yeats, Lady Gregory and J. M. Synge*. Ed. Ann Saddlemyer. Gerrards Cross: Colin Smythe, 1982.

Index